Strategies for the Threshold #7

Dealing with Azazel:

Spirit of Rejection

Anne Hamilton

Dealing with Azazel: Spirit of Rejection

Strategies for the Threshold #7

© Anne Hamilton 2021

Published by Armour Books

P. O. Box 492, Corinda QLD 4075

Cover Images: © Kevin Carden 'Father and Son in Battle'
| christianphotoshops.com; © Psychoshadow 'Recalling
Childhood' | canstockphoto.com; © iloveotto 'Asian Style
Textures' | canstockphoto.com

Section Divider Images: © cundrawan703 | canstockphoto.com

Interior Design and Typeset by Beckon Creative

ISBN: 978-1-925380-293

 A catalogue record for this
book is available from the
National Library of Australia

Note: Australian spelling and grammar conventions are used
throughout this book.

2024

Strategies for the Threshold #7

Dealing with Azazel:

Spirit of Rejection

Anne Hamilton

Other Books By
Anne Hamilton

Thank you

Alison	Linda
Colleen	Pauline
Donna	Quang
Elizabeth	Richard
Fiona	Ruth
Ian	Sarah
Janice	Shelagh
Joy	Terrie

Cornerstone Community, West Belfast

and especially my mum
who once again wrote
the prayers at the end
of each chapter

Contents

Introduction

MY SISTER WAS ONCE GIVEN A GOAT as a gift.

She'd gone to help a man whose vehicle had broken down on the side of the road and, as a reward for helping him, he gave her the goat he had with him. She brought it home and named it Giotto—after the famous medieval painter.

From the moment it arrived in our small backyard, one question loomed large: *What should we do about the goat?*

'Why didn't you give it straight back?' my mother asked, as she tied it to the clothes-line post. She was—not unnaturally—suspicious about the man's motives for off-loading the goat.

'That would have seemed ungrateful,' my sister said. 'I didn't want to be rude.'

Giotto's plaintive bleatings soon got on our nerves. They got on the neighbours' nerves as well. The goat was well-fed on grass and hay but its opportunities for wild foraging and frisking were severely limited. We had no fences on our boundary, just rock walls and a stand of bamboo, neither of which seemed much of a deterrent for a goat determined to chew through its rope and roam the suburban wilderness.

So Giotto remained, tied to the clothes-line post. We thought it might settle after a day or so. However, after the first two nights of incessant whining, keeping the whole family as well as the neighbours awake, the question—*What should we do about the goat?*— required an urgent, creative answer.

My mother, with more urgency than creativity, decided to lock Giotto overnight in a wardrobe in my brother's bedroom. This did not go well. The following day she received a phone call from his teacher who advised her to have a stern chat to her son about telling lies. 'He was asleep on the desk,' the teacher said, 'and when I told him he needed to discipline himself to stop watching late movies, he said he'd been kept awake all night by a goat trying to get out of his wardrobe.'

'Yes,' said my mother. 'That's right.'

The teacher was silent for a moment and then hung up. My mother wondered whether she'd suddenly been re-classified into the category of parent who defends their offspring, no matter what the truth actually is.

What should we do about the goat? It was a persistent and difficult question.

Eventually my mother found a farmer willing to take Giotto and so it was exiled out of suburbia and our lives. But the question, *'What should we do about the goat?'* is relevant, not just to our family at that time, but to everyone everywhere everywhen. The solution we found in real life for a lively young goat doesn't work so well for its spiritual counterpart—the spirit of rejection.

'What should we do about the goat?' When we fear rejection, which of the classic responses do we employ: fight, flight, freeze or flatter? Since none of them are genuinely effective, particularly when it comes to rejection's extreme form, scapegoating, what should we really do?

Does Scripture hold the answer? Jesus of course encountered the spirit of rejection. What did He do? As we look at His actions in these pages, let's uncover the answer to the question we all face regularly, whether we know it or not: *'What should we do about the goat?'*

Anne Hamilton
Brisbane, Australia 2021

PS: Many years ago, several leading scholars criticised the work of analysts who research the mathematical structure of ancient documents. The scholars dismissed the possibility of intentional arithmetic and geometric encoding on the basis, 'No one would do that!'

I immediately thought, 'But I *would!*' Their criticism wasn't informed by careful examination, it was simply an expression of their own bias. They thought such constraints would stifle creativity and couldn't imagine an artform fusing words and numbers.

So because I love mathematics and because I'm particularly interested in how it is used as a structural 'bed' in Scripture, I've used 'numerical literary design' in all my writing. Two of my books are exactly 77,777 words long. This is not one of them. However, it does have quite a few sections of 777 words or 888 words as well as 1743 words—a number which, for medieval writers, symbolised the kiss of heaven and earth.

1

The Art of Fear

Dean Ornish, clinical professor of medicine at the University of California, San Francisco, did a study on what happens when we are socially excluded. Subjects' brains responded the same way as if they'd experienced physical pain. Rejection doesn't just hurt like a broken heart; your brain feels it like a broken leg.

James Merritt, *52 Weeks Through The Psalms*

BACK WHEN I WAS A TEENAGER, I used to earn pocket money by baby-sitting. One night I was putting a sleepy toddler to bed when he opened one eye and said, 'I hate you.'

'No worries, little buddy,' I replied, as I tucked him in. 'I can handle rejection.'

That was the first time in my life I can remember specifically articulating the thought: *I can handle rejection.* And for years thereafter, that's what I said to myself whenever I was confronted by anything other than acceptance. *I'm not going to take this personally. I can handle rejection.*

You see, I always wanted to be a writer. Sometimes when I was baby-sitting and the children were all asleep, I'd work on the stories I was creating. I'd tweak the dialogue so it read more smoothly or I'd doctor the plotline to heighten the suspense. From the first, I knew I had to be able to handle rejection if I ever wanted to be published. It was, so I was told, part of the normal routine for a writer. Maybe I wouldn't ever be as devastated as the author who, with great anticipation, opened the stamped self-addressed return envelope only to discover the ashes of her manuscript inside, but it would still be a fact of life.

CS Lewis, it's alleged, was rejected 800 times before he sold a single piece of writing. Now eventually I decided that this number was a trifle unbelievable. Not because I didn't believe in his resilience but because his first volume of poems was printed when he was just twenty years old. If he'd had the benefit of email to be able to send out hundreds of messages to publishers easily and cheaply, it might be more credible. However his first publication came out in 1919 when even telephones were relatively uncommon.

So while Lewis turned out to be a doubtful case—at least to my mind—I knew there are many famous authors who could have produced the rejection slips as proof.

Novelist John Creasy received 753 rejections slips before going on to publish 564 books. Jack London, author of *Call of the Wild*, had over 600 rejections before making a sale. He apparently kept the first few year's worth on a single spike, and the museum in California devoted to his legacy has lots of them on display in a glass cabinet. Louis L'Amour, famous for his westerns, received over 200 rejections before his books went on to sell 330 million copies.

Chicken Soup for the Soul by Jack Canfield was rejected 144 times. From a massively popular book series, with about a dozen new titles each year, the company publishing these inspirational titles has branched out into television programming and pet food.

Margaret Mitchell's *Gone with the Wind* was rejected 38 times. It went on to win the Pulitzer Prize in 1937 and sell over 30 million copies.

James Patterson's first book was rejected 31 times. John Grisham's first book was rejected 28 times. Dr Seuss was rejected 27 times and Madeleine L'Engle's Newbery Award-winning *A Wrinkle in Time* 26 times.

All of these success stories exude the same theme—be persistent. Believe in yourself. Stay the course. Be resolved. Be determined.

Persevere. Don't take rejection personally.

I imbibed this advice, absorbed it into myself and never, for even a moment, suspected there was anything wrong with it. I repeatedly I told myself: *I can handle rejection.* Everything you read emanating out of the motivational scene tells you to pick yourself up after disappointment and try, try again. The advice is relentlessly similar: take as your role models those people who were resilient and who became overcomers through their tenacity.

Don't give up, even when the dream has died. That's the takeaway advice so many authors who have endured through the wilderness of disappointment will give aspiring fellow-writers.[1]

Think of all the people who would have forfeited greatness if they'd succumbed to the rejection they experienced. Consider, for just one, Abraham Lincoln.

He was defeated when he ran for the Illinois House of Representatives in 1832.

He was defeated when he ran for the U.S. House of Representatives in 1843.

He was defeated for the Senate in 1855.

He was defeated for Vice President in 1856.

He was defeated for the Senate again in 1858.

Did he let defeat define him? Of course not. Lincoln had a few successes in between these defeats and went on to be one of America's most famous presidents. He was elected in 1860, just two years after that last defeat for the Senate.

Or consider the critical moment when country and western singer Dolly Parton resolved she'd make it to the top. She revealed in her autobiography: 'My high school was small, so during graduation each of us got a chance to stand up and announce our plans for the future. "I'm going to junior college," one boy would say. "I'm getting married and moving to Maryville," a girl would follow. When my turn came I said, "I'm going to Nashville to become a star." The entire place erupted in laughter. I was stunned. Somehow, though, that laughter instilled in me an even greater determination to realise my dream. I might have crumbled under the weight of the hardships that were to come, had it not been for the response of the crowd that day. Sometimes it's funny the way we find inspiration.'

It was the mocking laughter and rejection of her dream that made Dolly more resolute. Did she tell herself, as I did, *I can handle rejection?* If she didn't, the vow she made to herself was powerful enough to push back on a mountain of let-downs and setbacks.

Or consider the prolific inventor, Thomas Edison, who is said to have tried and failed 1,000 times to invent the light bulb. Some stories vary the attempts to 3,000 or 6,000 or even 10,000. Probably none of these numbers are remotely true. In fact, the reported thousands of times Edison and his behind-the-scenes team—the 'muckers'—tried to perfect the light bulb is undoubtedly as exaggerated as those claims about CS Lewis and the number of rejections he is supposed to have experienced.

When it comes right down to it, the number of attempts Edison made is irrelevant. As is the number of rejections Lewis received. The purpose of these overblown details spread far and wide across the internet is, after all, *not* accuracy but encouragement.

Of course it's not just the messages on the internet that push you to believe in yourself. In bookstores, gift shops, cafes and kitchen walls, you'll find wonderful motivational memes, quotes and posters. Seminars, sermons and speeches all disseminate this kind of information to encourage you to never, ever, ever give up.

Some of it is accurate but most is not. But none of that matters. Because whether it's about a book, a relationship or a life calling, all of these uplifts are about soothing our wounded hearts when we're rejected and reinforcing our determination to make a comeback.

It took 27 years of hard work, perseverance, grit and determination for my first book to be traditionally published. I made lots of mistakes along the way, but I'm thankful for them, because I would never have learned certain spiritual principles otherwise. No one ever told me that the kind of encouragement I've just described is immensely dangerous. No one ever sat me down and advised me that, spiritually, very few things have the potential to be more damaging.

You see, the lesson I took out of all these heartening stories was this: rejection is an inevitable fact of life. Just pick yourself up, get over it, handle it, hang in there and shout, as Jack Canfield said that he did after each one of those 144 rejections of *Chicken Soup for the Soul*, 'Next!'

Now, let me be quite clear: it's indeed correct that rejection is an inevitable fact of life. It's also correct that we are called to overcome it.

But the issue is this: we're taught to think that 'overcoming' is thrusting the rejection aside and then persisting until we achieve the goal.

I never suspected anything was wrong with this until the day a couple of my friends asked me to give them some help concerning their own issues with rejection.

Let's back up a moment. This is the seventh book in a series specifically about strategies for passing over the threshold into our divine calling. However, if this is the first book you've read from the series, you may not be aware that a threshold is an astonishingly dangerous place. If I had to summarise the numerous and intricate threats associated with them, I'd do it with the two words the Holy Spirit gave me to describe their complexity: *threefold guard.*

In Scripture, we see the threefold guard at the resurrection—which is, by the way, one of the most wondrous threshold events of all time. The threefold guard there is composed of the watch, the stone and the seals.

The *watch* was the squad of Roman soldiers, the *stone* was the massive rock barring the entrance and the *seals* were placed by order of the governor and included curses to deter grave robbers. All of these were hindrances not only to getting in, but also to getting out.

In the spiritual world, as we are ready to pass over the threshold into our calling, we face a similar threefold guard. As believers who have received the resurrection power of Jesus, it's as if we have passed from death to life—but also as if we've somehow become trapped in the tomb. Our fears about heading out into the light are not baseless. We face terrifying angelic sentinels who have the legal right[2] to test us. Some of these cherubim and seraphim are helpful while others are hostile, and include fallen cosmic powers[3] such as Python, the spirit of constriction; Ziz, the spirit of forgetting; Leviathan/ Resheph, the spirit of retaliation; and Azazel, the spirit of rejection.

All these spirits are complex entities with multiple facets and functions to their natures. There's a tendency amongst believers towards ignoring the sophisticated character of these unholy spirits and reducing them to a single generalised role—Python, for example, is often seen as a spirit of divination,[4] while its wider agenda which includes constriction, ambiguity, flattery, intimidation and seduction is often overlooked.

The idea that angelic beings are simple with just one trick in their toolbox of temptation then leads us to an ever-increasing proliferation of spirits ranged against us. The list of demons grows ever longer as they acquire descriptive labels like the 'spirit of intimidation' or 'spirit of seduction' or 'spirit of jealousy'. However a familiarity with Python's modus operandi would enable us to recognise intimidation, seduction and jealousy as simply new tactics by one spirit rather present us with the daunting prospect that yet another entity has ganged up on us.

For several other examples—both forgetfulness and witchcraft are tools of Ziz; retaliation and mesmerism are part of Leviathan's agenda; and, as we shall see, both rejection and panic are under the operation of Azazel. Just as God has different faces, so these angelic majesties—fallen as they are—still mimic the Lord who created them and adopt different guises.[5] Nevertheless the 'spirit of panic' is not separate to the 'spirit of rejection'; they are one and the same.

This is very reassuring—at least it is, as far as I am concerned—because, often, when I analyse the life stories people tell me, I can see that they are under consistent attack by one spirit, not by a dozen lined up on multiple fronts. That realisation makes it so much easier to discern what will constitute an effective defence.

Now to return to our overview of the spirit of rejection, whenever you attempt to come into your calling—or even something that might conceivably have a remote connection to your calling—Azazel comes out swinging.

You can try to bind it, but that's not going to work permanently. In fact, binding might even be legal grounds for a retaliatory counter-strike. As I mentioned just three paragraphs ago, these are *angelic majesties.* You might baulk at that description but I'm simply quoting two of the earliest disciples: Jude, the brother of Jesus, and Peter, the Galilean fisherman who became one of the Lord's closest friends.

Jude makes a comparison between the disparaging attitude of some human believers with the prudent response of the archangel Michael to the satan:

> *Even the archangel Michael, when he disputed with the devil… did not presume to bring a slanderous charge against him, but said, 'The Lord rebuke you!'*

Jude 1:9 BSB

The apostle Peter makes a similar comment:

> *Although angels are more powerful than these evil beings, even the angels don't dare to accuse them to the Lord.*

2 Peter 2:11 CEV

Where did we get the idea we can routinely bind spirits? There is no record of Jesus binding any spirit.[6] He rebuked plenty. He cast out plenty. But we are told specifically when it comes to spirits like Leviathan, that binding is exceptionally unwise.[7] We might manage to do it once but we'll always remember the battle that ensued—and we'll never manage it a second time.

All too often 'binding' comes down to a reluctance to surrender our own power—power ultimately gifted by God. Our unwillingness to simply turn to Him and say, 'Can You please rebuke this?' is evidence of self-reliance. And when it comes to the spirit of rejection, we can't afford that defect in attitude.

'Miss, what is *wrong* with you?'

I glanced around my Year 11 Mathematics class as they sat, arms folded, glaring at me. 'What do you mean: *wrong*?'

'Your lessons have become so boring in the last few days,' one of the students volunteered. 'What's happened? You're no fun anymore.'

'Well...' I hesitated to reveal the truth. 'The principal has issued a directive that teachers are not allowed to be sarcastic any longer. I'm just following orders.'

Frowns appeared all around the room and various groups burst into animated discussion. Apparently I'd just allowed the students considerable insight into the mysterious change in atmosphere across quite a few of their classes.

Several minutes later, a delegation of three boys approached my desk. 'Miss,' they said, 'the principal doesn't understand how it is. There's a difference between being sarcastic at our expense and being sarcastic in general. You don't make *us* the butt of your jokes. We all like you the way you were. Please don't stop.'

I figured that, given such a heartfelt appeal, it was probably more important to obey the spirit of the principal's ruling rather than the letter of it. So I immediately reverted to my former self.

Some time later this same delegation of boys brought in a surprise for me at the end of one lesson. 'We couldn't find the perfect gift anywhere,' they said. 'We know you need a special button for your car, but here's some chocolates instead.'

'Thank you, gentlemen. What kind of special button does my car need?'

'Convert to broomstick.'

And off they hurried.

I thought about their parting comment for the rest of the day. It was so heavily nuanced it had obviously been worked on—very seriously—for quite some time. While at first sight it was a subtle insult, inviting offence and rejection, on a deeper level it was a test of relationship. What they wanted to know was how rigid the boundary line in the teacher-student power dynamic was.

Adolescents are at a time of life when they want to be independent. Many parents and teachers, rather than fostering this important aspect of maturity, all too often drive teenagers into rebellion. Sometimes this is done through harsh, immutably strict boundaries and sometimes it's done through the total abolition of boundaries.

Independence is a bilateral negotiation; rebellion is a unilateral declaration.[8] This is an incredibly important distinction. These boys felt secure enough in my class to push hard at the boundary line and risk the possibility of insult; they weren't trying to break the relationship and I don't have the slightest doubt they'd have apologised if they discovered they'd given offence. Rather they seriously wanted to learn how to negotiate with an adult—they wanted be seen as other than 'children'.

Rebellion and rejection are so closely entwined, it's worth recognising right now that passing over a threshold involves bilateral negotiations with God. Obedience is not mindless submission; it's an active, mature collaboration. The first thing Abraham did after raising a threshold covenant with God was negotiate for the fate of Sodom and Gomorrah—and while his efforts didn't make any difference in the long run, there are other stories recounted in Scripture where the intervention of a prophet did result in a different outcome.

In a world where total affirmation is increasingly demanded and where disagreement has become equal to rejection, it's worth remembering that God invites us to risk insulting Him as we *'reason together'*[9] about our differences, disagreements and disputes with Him.

He loves us enough to accept us just as we are. But He also loves us too much to accept that we should stay in the mire, just as we are.

Arguably the first person to experience rejection in the Bible is Cain. Okay, perhaps we could say it was Adam and Eve as they were expelled from Eden. But there's a critical difference between Cain and his parents. Because regardless of the events that occurred in the garden, Cain was the first person to actually receive God's advice when it comes to rejection.

> *The Lord accepted Abel and his gift, but he did not accept Cain and his gift. This made Cain very angry, and he looked dejected. 'Why are you so angry?' the Lord asked Cain. 'Why do you look so dejected? You will be accepted if you do what is right. But if you refuse to do what is right, then watch out! Sin is crouching at the door, eager to control you. But you must subdue it and be its master.'*

> Genesis 3:4–7 NLT

Now the mention of a door and sin stretched out across it—for that's the Hebrew sense of *crouching*—indicates this is indeed a threshold issue. In other words, it's all about Cain coming into his calling. The sin God mentions is attached to the feelings of dejection and rejection that Cain is experiencing—and God simply tells him that he has to *master* it.

Here we have the word of the Lord on the matter of rejection and the spirit that wants to control us through it: *master* it. *Subdue* it. Just do it.

Now easier said than done. I thought I had mastered rejection and I learned, to my surprise, that exactly the opposite was true. Ignoring the existence of rejection is not mastering it; it's simply side-stepping the entire issue. Still it was easy to fall for the delusion I had overcome it—especially when I compared myself with the rest of my family.

My dad struggled his entire life with feelings of rejection. And how did he deal with the fear associated with it? He simply rejected others before they rejected him. The spirit of rejection has this seductive way of saying, 'I am your *only* friend,' and he fell for that particular line time and time again.

My mum too has struggled all her life with rejection. She's different to my dad. How did she deal with the fear of rejection? Sometimes it was 'freeze in fright'—and sometimes it was 'flee into the night'. She could run from it. Or be stunned into silence by it. But, either way, somehow she always wound up accepting it. She too fell for the siren call of the spirit of rejection: 'I am your *only* friend.'

As I grew up, I watched both my parents and something deep inside me said: 'There's got to be a better way. With God's help, I can learn to overcome rejection. If you want to be an author, you can't afford to have a thin skin, girl. You gotta just deal with this.'

I thought I had it all sussed. And then a couple of friends who had terrible problems with rejection asked me to help them learn to subdue and master it. Now, as I said, that raised difficult questions. I wasn't exactly sure of the mechanism I used to overcome rejection. Yes, I knew that the breakthrough I'd experienced that had enabled me to cross the threshold into my calling was a result of dealing with my false refuge.[10] But there seemed to be more needed. After all, both my friends had worked through their false refuges but still had rejection issues.

Why didn't I have the same? I was at a loss to know how to help anyone else. When it came right down to it, I realised I'd distilled the essence of CS Lewis' 800 rejections and Thomas Edison's 1000 failures—never mind the accuracy of the numbers—and condensed the lesson down to: 'Don't take rejection personally. Just try again.'

Somehow, over time, that had become a life statement that fitted in with my vow—*I can handle rejection*—and it enabled me to feel the sting but let it go. Really, I just ignored rejection. I could acknowledge the disappointment but I didn't let it affect me. However, truth be told, I didn't know how I'd learned to do that.

I honestly didn't think that I could say to my friends, 'Just declare you can handle it,' and leave them with that. I thought of my dad's persistent efforts to cast rejection out of his life and knew, from his example, I would be telling them to paper over a core wounding. It would achieve nothing except deeper and more intractable rejection.

So, I went to God and said, 'I need Your help. I don't really have a clue how I handle rejection so successfully. So I can't help anyone else do it if I don't know how I manage it myself.'

There was silence for several seconds. Then God said to me: 'And just why would you want to teach anyone to handle rejection?'

You know those moments when you find you're holding your breath and your heart has stopped and a whirlwind has suddenly swept away every last coherent thought? It was one of those moments. As far as rebukes go, it was gentle and full of compassionate understanding but I grasped the nuances at once: *God doesn't think much of 'handling' rejection. It's no better than my dad's method of dealing with it. Or my mum's method either. In fact, I have a sense from His tone that He might think it's worse than either of them.*

My heart sank lower, if possible, than the soles of my boots.

If 'handling' rejection was not in fact mastering it or subduing it, what precisely did *overcoming* look like? How could I follow God's direction to Cain if I didn't know what it meant? The answer had to be in Scripture, but where? It was time to have a long heart-to-heart with Him and find out.

Let's begin with Jesus. We'll end with Him too, but without examining His life, we won't be able to identify the spirit of rejection. There's a trap in knowing the name of a spirit, rather than just being able to identify it as a descriptive label—but equally, ignorance of names is just as much of a snare. The especial trap in being able to identify a spirit by name is that *names are power.* If we haven't surrendered to Jesus our desire for power over our enemies, we'll be tempted to use their names to overcome them, rather than the name of Jesus of Nazareth.

Now Jesus was rejected many times in His life. Nevertheless, I still think it's possible to single out a particular moment when He confronted the specific spirit driving the exclusion He was subjected to. That moment occurred when He took His disciples to the northern border of Galilee to a locality known at the time as Caesarea Philippi and now called Banias.

> *When Jesus came to the region of Caesarea Philippi, He asked His disciples, 'Who do people say the Son of Man is?'*

They replied, 'Some say John the Baptist; others say Elijah; and still others, Jeremiah or one of the prophets.'

'But what about you?' He asked. 'Who do you say I am?'

Simon Peter answered, 'You are the Messiah, the Son of the living God.'

Jesus replied, 'Blessed are you, Simon son of Jonah, for this was not revealed to you by flesh and blood, but by My Father in heaven. And I tell you that you are Peter, and on this rock I will build My church, and the gates of Hades will not overcome it. I will give you the keys of the kingdom of heaven; whatever you bind on earth will be bound in heaven, and whatever you loose on earth will be loosed in heaven.' Then He ordered His disciples not to tell anyone that He was the Messiah.

Matthew 16:13–20 NIV

This is a very fraught passage theologically speaking, and I don't want to enter the centuries-long interdenominational war over whether the 'rock' Jesus built His church on was Peter himself or Peter's faith. All the battles which turn on the fine distinction between 'petros', *pebble*, and 'petra', *large mass of rock*, miss the real point as far as I am concerned: the name Jesus gave to Simon was actually *Cephas*. Peter is merely the closest Greek word to Hebrew Cephas—but it isn't an exact equivalent. In the cultural transition, it entirely glosses over some nuances that are critical to the nature of the 'rock' Jesus was referencing.

Cephas happens to be derived from 'kaph', one of the words for a *cornerstone*. It is related to 'kippur', *atonement*, and also to Caiaphas, the name of the high priest at the time. In addition, it is a pointer to the word for the *mercy seat* on the Ark of the Covenant. These are just some of the many profound ramifications within Jesus' gifting of the name Cephas—and, to include just one more, there is a subtle reference to the very day on which this declaration was made. Clues within the text indicate Jesus said this on Yom Kippur, the Day of Atonement.

Now, if you baulked at Peter and Jude's use of *'angelic majesties'* to describe fallen cosmic powers, you probably feel uncomfortable with Jesus giving Simon the name *'Cornerstone'*. This is to misunderstand the nature of the exchange between Simon and Jesus: it is a name covenant.[11] Simon gave to Jesus the divinely inspired title 'Messiah' and Jesus in turn offered Simon the name Cephas, *Cornerstone*. This interaction perfectly parallels the name exchange between God and Abram: God self-revealed as El Shaddai, inspiring Abram with a new name to use in addressing Himself, and then He gave to Abram a new destiny through a new name: Abraham.

When this type of transaction occurs on the human plane between ordinary people, the participants can only give to each other their own names—as, for example, in a wedding ceremony. Thus, one of the background aspects of this event at Caesarea Philippi is that Jesus was actually making a claim to be the Cornerstone referred to in Psalm 118.

The stone that the builders rejected has now become the cornerstone.

Psalm 118:22 NLT

He could call Simon *'Cornerstone'* because, as the Chief Cornerstone as well as the Name Above All Names, He retains the right to give to His friends any of His names. A very explicit example of this is when He calls Himself the *Light of the World*, but also calls and commands us to be the *Light of the World*.

Now the Chief Cornerstone is a rejected stone. And reinforcing this theme of being despised and cast aside were two significant factors: the time and the place of His announcement. It is no coincidence that the date was Yom Kippur, the Day of Atonement; still less was it a coincidence that Jesus had taken His disciples to the cultic enclosure of the Gates of Hell at Caesarea Philippi. There is colossal symbolism in His actions.

Back during the years the Israelites wandered in the wilderness, God had laid down some requirements for the Day of Atonement:

Aaron... must take the two male goats and present them to the Lord at the entrance of the Tabernacle. He is to cast sacred lots to determine which goat will be reserved as an offering to the Lord and which will carry the sins of the people to the wilderness of Azazel. Aaron will then present as a sin offering the goat chosen by lot for the Lord. The other goat, the scapegoat chosen by lot to be sent away, will be kept alive, standing before the Lord. When it is sent away to Azazel in the wilderness, the people will be purified and made right with the Lord.

Leviticus 16:6–10 NLT

Many commentators have grave difficulties in believing that God would instruct the Israelites to send off a scapegoat to carry away the sins of the people and deliver them to a fallen cosmic entity called Azazel. One goat for God and one goat for a demon?! This feels intrinsically wrong to so many believers that 'Azazel' has been interpreted in a variety of abstract ways: as a rocky cliff or a formless wandering. However, despite the wide variety of well-meaning theological objections to sending out the sin-laden scapegoat to a high-ranking goat-demon, I don't believe Jesus has left us the option of demythologising 'Azazel'. On the Day of Atonement He symbolised Himself as the scapegoat by going out into the wilderness to the shrine of a goat-demon.

The Gates of Hell at Caesarea Philippi were part of a cultic landscape dedicated to the Greek godling, Pan—a satyr or hybrid human-goat—who was considered to be the patron of flocks and herds.[12] Pan was worshipped by the Greeks as their defender in battle. He had, according to legend, caused their enemies, the Persians, to be overcome at the Battle of Marathon with mindless, frenzied fear—the wild rush of 'panic' which, in its very name, indicates its source in the activity of Pan.

In my view the actions of Jesus on the day of Yom Kippur enable us to identify Pan and Azazel as the same spiritual entity. The spirit of rejection and marginalisation is thus the spirit of panic. In addition, Jesus shows us the intimate link between the scapegoat and the cornerstone that the builders rejected.

This vital connection makes it possible for us to gain different insights on some well-known stories from the pages of Scripture. Let's go look at how Pan and Azazel use the art of fear to defeat us, even as we pass over the threshold and have attained the victory.

'Gazza, I want you to stay back.' As I let the class out for lunch, I turned to Gazza and directed him to the seat next to my desk. It was going to be a tough talk and I was already sighing internally and praying earnestly for help. Gazza had just failed Year 8 algebra, the only person in nearly three hundred students to do so. He sat down and looked at his feet.

'Gazza,' I said, 'I don't like to think what I'm thinking. The last test we did in algebra, you were the only person in all of ten classes to get 100%. Now you're the only person to fail. I don't like to be suspicious but, Gazza, I think you miscalculated.'

Gazza raised his head. He'd been a very average student until, to everyone's stunned amazement including his own, he'd topped that algebra test.

I looked him in the eye. 'I think you miscalculated *badly*. You didn't mean to fail. You just meant to get a very ordinary score that would get your friends off your back. I know they've accused you of cheating—but, if you're the only person to score 100% last time, you can't have cheated. Who got the same as you? No one. So *I* know you didn't cheat. I think you got so scared your friends would reject you if you got 100% a second time, that you *deliberately* chose to answer some questions incorrectly.'

I handed a new test paper to Gazza. 'You've got a choice,' I told him. 'I hope you will choose the way of courage and be who you really are. But it's up to you if your friends are more important. You can redo the test right now and no one will know your score except you and me. Or you can go to lunch and come back to class tomorrow as if nothing has happened. I'll have some extra worksheets to get you up to scratch.'

Gazza took out his biro, looked over the test and handed it back in record time. 'Thanks, miss,' he said. They were the only words he spoke during the entire rebuke.

I checked his work. 'You're going to have to do better next time,' I told him as I waved him off. 'You've only got 99%.'

Gazza had been desperately afraid. His mates had turned on him. In fact, they didn't care in the least about cheating; they cared he'd betrayed their unspoken code of mediocrity. On the outside, Gazza displayed a don't-care attitude, on the inside he was frantic not to be rejected, so he sacrificed himself for acceptance.

Such sacrifices bring us into complicity with the spirit of rejection. These tacit agreements with the enemy reinforce any covenants our ancestors raised. Instead of revoking our unholy covenants, we express our unity with them.

The Biblical story that features complicity with fear and panic most prominently is, in my view, that of Elijah. Just a few days before he faced off with the prophets of Baal, he'd come back from Lebanon.[13] Travelling through the drought-stricken dustbowl of Samaria and looking for King Ahab, he met up with Obadiah, the palace steward. Now Obadiah was extremely reluctant to become Elijah's errand boy. He knew Ahab had a tendency to shoot the messenger if things didn't work out, so he wasn't willing to risk his life if Elijah was about to perform a vanishing act.

So, in an effort to persuade Elijah to commit to meeting the king, Obadiah made a significant revelation: holed up in two caves were a hundred prophets, faithful to Yahweh. Obadiah was secretly supplying them with bread and water.

Events moved quickly once Obadiah was persuaded to go get the king. Shortly afterwards, Elijah was on top of Mount Carmel confronting the prophets of Baal and Asherah. Ahab and his court as well as an assembly of the people of Israel were in attendance. In a stunning demonstration,

Baal was shown as impotent and Yahweh as the true ruler of heaven. The prophets of Baal were shown to serve a feeble storm deity uninterested in responding to the sacrifices of his worshippers. By the end of the day, fire had descended from heaven onto a stone altar, the prophets of Baal were dead and Elijah had dashed down the mountain ahead of Ahab's chariot in an attempt to outrace the storm wind plunging out of heaven.

In summary: the drought was over, the prophets of Baal had been removed, Jezebel's power base was broken, the psychological moment for a palace coup was perfect. All Elijah needed to do in order to change the government of Samaria was ask Obadiah to usher the one hundred prophets of Yahweh out of the caves and into the court.

This was, as I think it is possible to discern from the breadcrumb trail of clues, precisely what God wanted. He wanted His faithful ones, who happened to be ideally positioned to replace the deposed false prophets who had been Ahab and Jezebel's cabinet members, congressional representatives and deep state operatives, to be taken out of hiding and brought into the light.

But it didn't happen. Instead Jezebel issued a death threat.

> *'May the gods deal with me, be it ever so severely, if by this time tomorrow I do not make your life like that of one of them.'*

> 1 Kings 19:2 NIV

And at that point, Elijah panicked. Many commentators point out he seems to have slipped into deep depression. One of the most important features of depression is an inward focus, rather than an outward or, even more significantly, an upward focus. In his exhaustion, Elijah was distracted and so he entirely forgot the power of fire, wind and water God had just displayed. Fearing for his life, he fled the kingdom. *Mindless* is an apt description of his behaviour. It covers both his sudden lack of memory and his wild, flustered flight.

For a long time, his reaction to Jezebel's death threat didn't quite make sense to me. After all, Elijah had been subject to this kind of menacing behaviour for years. It's why he left Samaria to hide out in the Brook Cherith and then later to take refuge in Zarephath. So he knew he would be facing death threats and sudden dangers to his life in coming back. In addition, God sent him reassurance through an unexpected surprise: *he wasn't alone*. He had support and allies close at hand— Obadiah, for one, and the hundred prophets who had remained steadfast in their loyalty to Yahweh.

So what is there about Jezebel's threat that is so terrifying Elijah goes into a mental tailspin and abandons all hope that God will save him unless he flees as quickly as possible and as far as possible? After scrutinising her words for a very long time, I've finally reached the conclusion that the words that unnerve Elijah are simply '...the gods...'

Who are these spiritual rulers that Jezebel invoked? Well, given that she worshipped Asherah, I'd say it's fairly safe to suggest that she'd summoned the 'young lions', the sons of the goddess, who were brothers to the storm god, Baal Hadad, the so-called 'cloud-rider'. It was likely Baal Hadad the rain-bringer was the particular 'baal' worshipped by the prophets on Mount Carmel. They slashed themselves diligently—and perhaps to express blood covenant—in an attempt to elicit a response from him. So it makes sense Jezebel would call on his brother-spirits to avenge the death of his prophets. These sons of the goddess were seventy in number.

Apparently seventy godlings were far too much for Elijah. He did a runner. Fleeing south, out of Samaria and into the kingdom of Judah, he didn't stop until he reached Beersheba. There he dismissed his servant. Travelling on, he prayed to die. Instead he met an angel, ate the food the heavenly messenger prepared for him and, in the strength of that sustenance, journeyed for forty days—until he reached Horeb, the mountain also known as Sinai.

As Moses had done before him, Elijah hid himself in a cleft in the rocks. Coming out, he experienced a fire, an earthquake, a whirlwind—and a silence. God was not in the earthquake or the wind or the fire, but out of the silence He spoke in a still, small Voice.

Now let's make no mistake about what happens next. We've been conditioned to read *with* the designated hero in Scripture and *against* the hero's opponents, whatever truth they are speaking to power. Thus we actually miss noticing abuse and the seeds of abuse. And although I won't be looking at the spirit of abuse until a later volume in this series, I want to signal that this spirit can begin its infiltration of our lives even when we're close to God.

Thus let us read *with* the *text*, not with the hero. In this case, Elijah. When God speaks to Elijah, He delivers a rebuke. A subtle and gentle rebuke, full of compassion and understanding. But it's still a rebuke.

> *There he came to a cave and lodged in it. And behold, the word of the Lord came to him, and He said to him,* **'What are you doing here, Elijah?'**
>
> *He said,* **'I have been very jealous for the Lord, the God of hosts. For the people of Israel have forsaken Your covenant, thrown down Your altars, and killed Your prophets with the sword, and I, even I only, am left, and they seek my life, to take it away.'**
>
> *And He said, 'Go out and stand on the mount before the Lord.' And behold, the Lord passed by, and a great and strong wind tore the mountains and broke in pieces the rocks before the Lord, but the Lord was not in the wind. And after the wind an earthquake, but the Lord was not in the earthquake. And after the earthquake a fire, but the Lord was not in the fire. And after the fire the sound of a low whisper, a thin silence. And when Elijah heard it, he wrapped*

his face in his cloak and went out and stood at the entrance of the cave.

*And behold, there came a Voice to him and said, **'What are you doing here, Elijah?'***

*He said, **'I have been very jealous for the Lord, the God of hosts. For the people of Israel have forsaken Your covenant, thrown down Your altars, and killed Your prophets with the sword, and I, even I only, am left, and they seek my life, to take it away.'***

And the Lord said to him, 'Go, return on your way to the wilderness of Damascus. And when you arrive, you shall anoint Hazael to be king over Syria. And Jehu the son of Nimshi you shall anoint to be king over Israel, and Elisha the son of Shaphat of Abel-meholah you shall anoint to be prophet in your place. And the one who escapes from the sword of Hazael shall Jehu put to death, and the one who escapes from the sword of Jehu shall Elisha put to death. Yet I will leave seven thousand in Israel, all the knees that have not bowed to Baal, and every mouth that has not kissed him.'

1 Kings 19:9–18 ESV

Notice the emphasis on the repeated question and repeated answer. Was God giving Elijah a chance to seriously reflect on the veracity of his statement? After all, he was moaning about the people turning against God—when, in fact, they'd just turned back to Him. All

God's prophets had *not* been slaughtered—a hundred of them were hidden in two caves. And how would the king's steward Obadiah feel about Elijah's complaint that he was the only faithful servant left?

No doubt the spirit of forgetting had found Elijah easy prey.[14] Still, the spirit of panic reinforced his excuses and his memory reshuffle.

When Elijah gave the same self-justifying answer a second time, God basically told him he could retire. There were just three tasks to be completed first. None of these involved returning to Samaria and facing Jezebel. Elijah could simply head up the ancient King's Highway through Damascus, anoint Hazael, then come back to Ramoth Gilead where Jehu was stationed, anoint him, and lastly return to his hometown of Tishbe, anointing Elisha in a nearby village on the way.

Now, once He'd given Elijah this assignment, God could have reminded him of those hundred prophets Obadiah was sheltering but He went one better: He revealed the existence of seven thousand followers loyal to Himself. This is a sizeable number, because it matches the strength of Ahab's army.[15]

Did Elijah realise at that moment how monumentally he'd failed? You see, God was telling him—obliquely it's true—that His faithful remnant outnumbered the young lions of Asherah by one hundred to one. Moreover, if those seven thousand had been divided into bands headed up by one of each of the hundred prophets, there would have been seventy in each band.

Seventy: that's not just *any* old number. It tells us that God had indeed intended a change of government. But because of Elijah's obstinacy, His will was not being done on earth as it was in heaven.

The governments of this world—particularly those in the western world—are increasingly prioritising laws to compel the affirmation of life choices contrary to Scripture. In addition, they are proposing extreme penalties for expressing views that are the historical norm. Hate speech is outlawed, even while what is 'hateful' has no clear definition, but depends entirely on the eye or the ear of the beholder.

Today's 'cancel culture' thinks it will change the world simply by silencing the opposition. It won't. Because the problem with passing laws to enforce affirmation and to criminalise hate speech is that, in far too many instances, the real heart of the issue is self-rejection. Not rejection by those who have different views but *self*-rejection. When this is the most crucial part of the dynamic, there can never be enough positive affirmation, never enough compliments, never enough encouragement. Ever. Affirmation does not eject rejection; it merely provides a temporary 'fix' to salve the wound. It also creates an insatiable consumer, insistently demanding *more* and *better* approval.

My mother once prayed for a woman who, as a child, had always been affirmed by her parents and teachers. She had been invariably praised for her efforts, regardless of their quality.

'How blessed you were!' my mother exclaimed, thinking of her own struggles to overcome rejection in her life.

'Blessed?' The woman was vehement. 'I was *cursed!'*

'What do you mean?' my mother asked.

'As soon as I left school, I discovered that life's not like that. I've been in therapy for over four decades as a result.'

The first time this woman was told to smarten up in her first job and redo some of her work to a better standard, she collapsed mentally. No one had ever told her previously that her efforts were not up to scratch. No one had ever said before that her performance was 'not good enough'. She had no resilience built into her as a child; no clue as to how to look at a piece of work and find its flaws, let alone fix them; no way of coming back emotionally from a negative assessment. Her first rejection was so devastating she was in counselling, still trying to come to terms with it—as well as many subsequent ones—nearly half a century later.

Total affirmation is as much a wrecking ball as total rejection. Both lead to a no-win scenario. Whenever the spirit of rejection is afflicting a person, then the partner of that person is always in a double bind. Whether they affirm the person or not, the spirit of rejection is the only one who wins.

Vince was oppressed by the spirit of rejection. He worked hard to get a promotion, sacrificing time with his wife and family. However, he lost out to someone less experienced and less qualified. Nothing his wife said or did assuaged the sense of rejection he experienced. His complicity with Azazel was in fact reinforced.

So he worked still harder and eventually he got that coveted promotion. His wife praised him so exuberantly and Vince felt so good, he had to work even harder. He desperately needed to experience that brief glow of approval again. So his time with his wife and family was reduced even further. The next time he got a promotion, his wife was wary, wondering if it meant still less attention from Vince. She didn't celebrate it as she did previously. So Vince thought to himself: 'I must work even harder to be recognised.'

Ultimately in a case like this, Vince's sense of rejection plays right into the hands of Azazel, and it doesn't matter whether his wife affirms him or not. The outcome will be the same. He will work harder and, in the process, reject his wife and family as well as set up the perfect cauldron of resentment that ensures the next generation will perpetuate the agreement with Azazel he's modelled for them.

When governments choose to deal with the issues that involve societal rejection—of whatever kind—by deciding they are the experts on who needs affirmation and how they need it, they are actually only deepening the problem. We have reached the point where eugenic experimentation on children is now routinely recommended as the only available option in many instances which would once have been successfully treated with counselling. The long-term results of such hormonal, chemical and surgical alterations are completely unknown, but that hasn't given our governments pause. The idea of exploiting children and subjecting them to the callous agendas of adults is, of course, hardly new.

Last century, the Nazi regime committed the same sort of atrocities and abuse.

When it comes to a consideration of government, the number *seventy* is extremely significant—and not just because of those fallen angels called the 'young lions'. Since the dispersal of peoples from the Tower of Babel, *seventy* in Jewish culture symbolised both the 'number of nations' and the 'number of government'. In Genesis 10, the list of seventy descendants of Noah through Shem, Ham and Japheth is seen as a tabulation of the nations.

So, by noting that God had reserved seven thousand loyal Israelites for Himself as well as one hundred prophets, we can surmise exactly what His plan was. We can look back on the breaking of the drought and the onrush of the wind from heaven at Mount Carmel and realise this: God wanted bands of seventy disciples taking the good news of change throughout Samaria and teaching the people how to renew the covenant with Yahweh.

And because of Elijah's panicked flight, this didn't happen for over eight hundred years when Jesus sent a band of seventy disciples through Samaria to do exactly that. Yes, Jesus finished the job Elijah had been tasked with bringing to fulfilment.

The spirit of panic had so overwhelmed Elijah that the propitious moment for the completion of this assignment passed by. That's what this spirit wants to achieve in our own lives too—to ruin our chances to seize the best opportunities as they arise. Now this is not to say God won't give us second chances. In fact, in the story of Elijah, God still wanted a change in the government of Samaria. And He still wanted Elijah to be part of the outworking of this change. Less to the forefront, sure, but that should have suited Elijah. After all, he'd made it clear he wanted out.

God basically agreed to his retirement, providing he still facilitated that change in government by anointing Jehu, anointing Hazael and anointing Elisha. Two new kings and a personal successor.

But did Elijah do as God asked? Concerning Elisha, maybe. If throwing a mantle qualifies as 'anointing'. But regarding Jehu and Hazael? No. At first Elijah simply procrastinated. Years eventually went by as he delayed, dawdled and deferred obedience. He never did anoint either of them. It was only a considerable time after he'd ascended to heaven that one of the sons of the prophets finally anointed Jehu. And although his successor Elisha many years later met Hazael in Damascus and informed him he would be king, it is not recorded that he anointed him.

Elijah did not end well. We tend to think he did because, as I said, we're conditioned to read with the hero, not with the text. But he spent his last years in defiance of God.

Jesus told a story once about two sons. One said to his father, 'No, I'm not going to do what you want,' but then changed his mind and did it anyway. The second son said, 'Yes, father, I'm on it right away,' but never did anything at all. Was the second son in the story modelled on Elijah—the one who started out so well but then just gave up? The one who left so much undone and who wasted so many divinely sent opportunities. Elijah defied God—there's no way of softening that reality. He was headstrong and rebellious—apparently he thought he knew better than God who should be king. His actions seem to indicate that, in his view, Ahab—for all his faults and weaknesses—was a more malleable option than his violent, uncouth battle commander, Jehu. And Ben-Hadad, who was willing to make a treaty with Israel, was a softer option than the brutal Hazael.

Had Elijah not so steadfastly procrastinated for so long, the tragedy of Naboth's Vineyard would not have occurred. His choice not to complete the task God had assigned to him—to anoint Jehu—meant that Ahab and Jezebel ruled for years longer than heaven intended.

Naboth's Vineyard was right next to Ahab's palace on the hill of Samaria. Ahab wanted it for a garden and when Naboth refused to sell his inheritance, Jezebel hired a couple of 'sons of Belial' to falsely accuse Naboth of blasphemy and treason. They said he'd cursed both God—or perhaps 'the gods'—and the king. Belial, the spirit of abuse, would not have had this opportunity except for Elijah's disobedience.

Now, after Naboth's death, Elijah prophesied to Ahab that dogs would lick Jezebel's remains by the wall of Jezreel—which, in the fullness of time, turned out to be the garden which had formerly been Naboth's Vineyard. And, hearing a similar fate pronounced for himself, Ahab repented.

Years went by, and Jehu finally came to the throne. When he did, Jehu reminded his officer Bidkar they'd been riding behind Ahab when Elijah had prophesied dogs would lick Jezebel's blood in Naboth's vineyard. 2 Kings 9:25 indicates Elijah was actually in Jehu's presence but, far from seizing the opportunity to obey God's instructions, he let it slip.

The spirit of panic got such a hold on Elijah's life he rejected God's plan for him and his nation. Rejection and panic ally themselves with the spirit of forgetting and the spirit of abuse, and they work together to undo the good that we do.

What did Elijah fear most? Not God, not Ahab and not even Jezebel. What he feared was the seventy 'young lions', the sons of the goddess Asherah. These cosmic spirits were said to have their palatial residences on a summit in the far north of Israel: the Mount of Assembly.

This is, I believe, triple-peaked Hermon and it is also my understanding it is the 'high mountain' Jesus climbed with James, John and Simon, who'd just been newly-minted as Cephas. It is no coincidence that Elijah appeared there, right in the stronghold of the enemies he most feared. What he could not withstand in his own lifetime, he could face in the company of Jesus.

Prayer

The prayers in this book are given as guidelines and jumping-off points for your own interaction with God. I therefore strongly recommend they are read through carefully *before* being prayed aloud with intentionality. If you feel a check in your spirit from the Holy Spirit about any aspect of the prayer, then heed it. Put off praying until you receive permission from God.

It is vitally important to recognise that prayer is about relationship with the Father. None of the words here are intended as a formula and to use them that way is to abuse them. The prayers are nothing in themselves; they are not powerful or guaranteed; they are meant as a start, not as an end in themselves. Power comes from Jesus alone, not from any cleverly—or even wisely—crafted petitions.

Because, however, of the importance of *honour* in prayer (discussed in the previous book in the series), each prayer starts with a variation on the theme, 'Hallowed be Your Name'. The shift from dishonour to honour is only possible as we hold onto the hem of Jesus' prayer shawl and ask Him to mediate before the Father for us. In the end, prayer is all about Him!

Father God: in all that I think and do and say, I ask that I keep and speak Your name in honour, holiness and respect. I pledge to honour You in my words, thoughts and actions. Correct me, Father, when I fail to respect you. May this prayer be brought before You like sweet incense. Teach me what holiness means. There are so many ways in which I dishonour You—the times when, like Elijah, I think I know better than You do about me and what is best for me.

Remind me, Father, that You know me far better than I know myself. I repent of deposing You from Your rightful place in my life. I repent of rejecting You, Father, and refusing Your will. I repent of my arrogance and pride and I ask Your forgiveness. I ask Jesus of Nazareth to empower these words of repentance through the cogency of His blood that was shed on the Cross for the forgiveness of my sins.

Yahweh, You know me and love me. As a child, my will was broken by harsh discipline and violent words. All my life I have felt rejection as I fled any possible re-occurrence of the cruelty I experienced and the shame I suppressed. I lied, Father, when I smiled and said it didn't hurt and that it didn't matter. It did not take long for that lie to become a bigger lie: 'I'm not hurting. I don't matter.'

In believing that, I dishonoured You and myself. By agreeing to the lie, I was untrue to myself and false to You. And in being untrue to myself, it was not possible to be true to others. I repent of lying and agreeing with the lie. I repent of fleeing the pain of rejection.

I realise that the only way to overcome rejection is to stand strong and face Azazel. I ask for the strength of Jesus to say, 'I stand here heart to heart and hand in hand with the Lord Jesus Christ and, with Him by my side, I ask for mastery of rejection to control my thoughts, words and actions. May the Lord rebuke you.'

And to Jesus I say: 'Thank You for always being here for me. I am nothing without You but, with You by my side, I can be an overcomer.'

In the name of Jesus, the finisher of our faith.

Amen.

2

The Art of Roar

There is fear and intolerance in pride; it is insensitive and uncompromising. The less promise and potency in the self, the more imperative is the need for pride. The core of pride is self-rejection.

Bruce Lee

I COULD CHOOSE ANY ONE of hundreds of stories involving rejection and family, friends or colleagues but, in general, I'm going to choose stories from Scripture. The reason for this is very simple: we have sufficient detail in so many accounts that we actually can tell what was *supposed* to have happened, had the heroes chosen otherwise.

The Chronicles of Narnia features this interchange between the Great Lion, Aslan, and the timid-and-yet-contrawise-intrepid Lucy:

'To know what would have happened, child?' said
Aslan. *'No. Nobody is ever told that.'*

'Oh dear,' said Lucy.

CS Lewis, *Prince Caspian*

I disagree that we are never told what *would* have
happened. I believe the stories we have about the life
of Jesus are illuminations, time and time again, about
God's ideal plan for history—and that Jesus brought
that plan to fruition in specific seasons and localities to
show us what was meant to have happened in the past.

Our conditioning to read with the hero means we tend
to equate his actions with God's will. Consider, for
example, Nehemiah. If we put the books of the Hebrew
Scriptures in chronological order, his story timewise
would be the very last. The book of Nehemiah, the
king's cupbearer who masterminded the rebuilding
of the walls of Jerusalem, ends with the exclusion of
foreign women and the decree to forbid intermarriage.
From the book of Ezra we learn that the men of Israel
divorced their foreign wives and sent them away, along
with any children born within the marriage.

Across the centuries, the God-fearing integrity of
Nehemiah and Ezra has led to ethnic discrimination and
racial prejudice—because we've judged their sincerity
as righteousness and as indicative of the correctness of
their views. We haven't looked to see God's commentary
on their behaviour: His annotations in the margins that

are only visible in the actions of Jesus. When Jesus went to the well in Sychar and met a much-married, excluded, foreign woman—perfectly representative of the kind of woman Nehemiah banished—He asked her for a drink. *He effectively asked her to be the cupbearer to the King of the world:* and, in the most subtle of ways, He denounced the actions of Nehemiah and Ezra.

What *should* they have done? They should have given the women in their own time the choice of Rahab, Ruth, Zipporah and Bithiah: covenant with us to become part of Israel. *Graft yourself into us,* that's what they should have said. *Don't cut our men off from the vine of Israel and lead them astray as the wives of Solomon and Ahab did to their husbands. Choose to cut covenant if you want to stay: promise you will give up other worship and serve only the God of Israel.*

This is just one of numerous examples from the life of Jesus where His work of healing history and binding up the wounds of the past also forms a discreet commentary on the actions of various kings and governors, rulers and warriors. One of my favourite examples is His time-out, over the last winter of His life, in a refuge in Gilead.

Now the eleventh chapter of the Book of Hebrews honours, amongst others, the faith of Jephthah, one of Israel's early judges—famous for making a rash vow about sacrificing the first thing out of his door if he was victorious in battle. However, by spending two months on the hills of Gilead, Jesus instead directed our attention to Jephthah's *daughter* and honoured *her.*[16]

So let's turn our attention now to the other person who conversed with Jesus when He appeared with Elijah on the Mount of Transfiguration. That was, of course, Moses.

Now, if Elijah had rejection issues, they are mere sandcastles compared to the soaring Himalayan range of problems Moses never conquered. There's a purpose in scrutinising the life of Moses so closely: we will be able see, in his story, the *generational* outworking of rejection.

Now, as the Book of Exodus opens, the Israelites are enslaved in Egypt. The Pharaoh at the time wasn't getting much satisfaction from the pair of midwives he'd told to kill newborn Hebrew boys, so he commanded his people to take matters into their own hands and throw any male babies into the Nile—a river infested with crocodiles, cobras, mambas, vipers, monitor lizards and hippos.

Jochabed, the mother of Moses, nevertheless decided that the river was the safest place.

> *She got him a papyrus basket and coated it with tar and pitch. Then she placed the child in the basket and set it among the reeds along the bank of the Nile. And his sister stood at a distance to see what would happen... Soon the daughter of Pharaoh went down to bathe... She saw the basket among the reeds... When she opened it, she saw the child... Then his sister said... 'Shall I go and call one of the Hebrew women to nurse the child for you?' 'Go ahead,' Pharaoh's daughter told her. And the girl went and called the boy's mother. Pharaoh's*

daughter said to her, 'Take this child and nurse him for me...' So the woman took the boy and nursed him. When the child had grown older, she brought him to Pharaoh's daughter, and he became her son. She named him Moses and explained, 'I drew him out of the water.'

Exodus 2:3–10 BSB

Reeds are plants that grow on riverbanks or lakesides and delineate the land from the water. They mark a threshold—in fact, such an important threshold that the Hebrew word for *reeds* rhymes with the word for *threshold*. But this threshold was incredibly hostile. And what was imprinted on the heart of this tiny vulnerable child, Moses, adversely affected his entire life, his generational stream and centuries of Israelite history.

Most people look at Moses and see a hero of the faith, a mighty deliverer, the meekest man of all time—a legend beyond his own lifetime, the champion who achieved such god-like status in the eyes of his nation that Jesus actually had to tell the people in His own era Moses wasn't the one who provided the manna from heaven![17]

Instead, let's look at Moses, the very flawed and wounded human being, the man who never recovered from that first traumatic threshold. It's widely recognised that what's written into the hearts of children, even before birth, can rule their lives—infants might not have language but nonetheless they can sense rejection and abandonment, fear and rage. So Moses might not have had the words for crocodiles, cobras, mambas, vipers, monitor lizards, hippos or for a homicidal Pharaoh who was about to become his grandfather by adoption, but he'd have imbibed the hostility of the environment around him.

We can be sure that is true because of his later actions surrounding thresholds.

When Moses fled Egypt because he'd killed a taskmaster who was beating a Hebrew slave, he shepherded in the land of Midian for forty years. He married Zipporah, the daughter of a local priest, and he was in the middle of another ordinary day in the desert when he saw a burning bush. When he went to look, the angel of the Lord spoke to him.

Now, something very important happened in this encounter that's easy to overlook: God offered Moses a new name.

Just as God gave new names to Abram, Sarai, and to Jacob to indicate their new destiny and calling, so—unsurprisingly—He offered a new name to Moses. And just as God revealed a new name for Himself, El Shaddai, just prior to renaming Abram and Sarai; so here again at the burning bush, He revealed a new name for Himself.

I Am Who I Am is a name that had never been known before. God was offering a name exchange, very similar to the one that, in a later age, would see Simon renamed as Cephas. This wasn't just an exchange, it was a covenant and, as such, it involved a sharing of secrets. God asked

Moses to accept a redefinition of his own name, a new meaning for it hidden in the question: '*What is that* you have in your hand?'

'*What is that?*' is actually wordplay on the name Moses. In Hebrew, this is Moshe, and is related to *messiah*. God's question, 'What is that?' is 'mazeh',[18] a rhyme for Moshe. Under normal circumstances, this wouldn't mean much at all. But as God changed what was in Moses' hand from a shepherd's staff to a serpent back to a staff, He proclaimed a new destiny and showed Moses what his life has been heading towards. The shepherd's staff said he is able to survive in the wilderness, guiding a flock of sheep in safety through the desert; the serpent[19] symbolises the cobra on the front of Pharaoh's crown, indicating Moses is also able to negotiate the protocols of a royal court. Yet the return to the shape of a staff revealed God's ultimate calling: the Hebrew word for *staff* is also the word for *tribe*. So, God was effectively saying to Moses, 'The tribes of Israel are in your hands. Just as you can guide a flock of sheep safely here, so you can guide the people.'

God was offering Moses a new name because, after all, Moses isn't a Hebrew word, but an Egyptian one, *drawn from the water*. And while it was nonetheless prophetic of Moses' calling to lead a people who would be *drawn from the waters of the sea*, but it's not the fullness that God wanted.

Now, this may be a surprise but Moses turned God down. In fact, he turned Him down, by my count, five times in this scene alone[20] and well over twelve thousand times more during the next forty years. Yes, twelve *thousand*. God, slow to anger, abounding in love and faithfulness, finally gave way after four decades and basically said, 'Ok, your loyalty to Pharaoh's daughter is commendable. Keep the name. Let's just rework it a bit. Instead of *drawn from the water*, can it be *water drawn from the Rock?*'

But Moses couldn't even do that. It's one thing to take a man out of Egypt but entirely another to take Egypt out of the man.

Moses never said 'yes' to God; he never accepted the reworking of his name that God offered him. With just a subtle bit of poetic nuancing, God offered to turn an Egyptian name into a Hebrew one. But Moses turned Him down time and time again. And in refusing the name covenant, he also turned down the threshold covenant and friendship with God. Abraham had become a Friend of God and this was same gift offered to Moses. But he rejected it.

Now can we be sure Moses rejected it? I believe we can. When, reluctantly, he left Mount Sinai and travelled down to Egypt with his wife and son, he entered a lodging place and there God tried to kill him.[21] This is one of the most mysterious episodes in all of Scripture. Why on earth would God attempt to kill the very person He's just appointed to go to Pharaoh and say, 'Let My people go'?

Fact is, hidden in the Hebrew is the information that the lodging place Moses entered was a place of treachery. Moses had betrayed God. It doesn't say how, but we can guess. The story offers some subtle clues that threshold covenant violation and rejection were involved.

Up until the end of the nineteenth century, in many countries around the world, a threshold covenant came into existence simply by crossing a threshold. It was an ordinary, everyday part of life but it also carried sacred meaning. In the ancient world, particularly for sojourners in the desert, hospitality was a vital aspect of the culture. It was essential to survival in a hostile environment. Even a chieftain's enemies could be offered hospitality under very specific conditions. And those conditions were simply that the enemy passed over the cornerstone in the doorway: the cornerstone was not simply a threshold, it was an altar.

So, it seems Moses covenanted with a foreign idol. That wouldn't have been hard to do if, for example, he chose to enter a desert shrine dedicated to a spirit of the wilderness. This was the sixth time Moses said 'no' to God and this time it was like a stab in the back: God had offered Moses a name and threshold covenant and all the benefits that went with it, but Moses had preferred to take up with some minor godling. What Moses was apparently counting on was this: since the obligations of a threshold covenant include protection and defence against all-comers, then this godling would guard him against Yahweh, just in case Yahweh still wasn't willing to take 'no' for an answer. Moses wasn't just threatening to derail the Exodus before it even started, he was quite possibly about to find himself obligated to bring the Israelites out into the desert to worship at this shrine in the wilderness. In fact, Moses had set up the situation in such a way that God didn't have any real option but to kill him. Just to prove that the covenantal defence of any other so-called god wouldn't save him.

Think about that.

Now you probably wouldn't credit that, in this day and age, believers would be so terrified of the call of God on their lives that they'd act like Moses and try to covenant with some other spirit for protection. However I've been rendered speechless to find there are people who have done exactly this.

Our first reaction to the call of God should in fact be just like Moses: we should indeed think, 'Impossible! I *can't* do that! I just *can't*.' But our second reaction should be: 'But, with You, Lord, nothing is impossible.' Yet some people are so reluctant to surrender to God they are scared stiff of any divine calling that lies beyond their own strength.

Now fortunately for Moses, his wife Zipporah had the sense to realise that, to save his life, the covenant with God had to be reaffirmed. She did this by circumcising someone—it's unclear whether it was Moses himself or his son. And straight after this, Moses said 'no' for a seventh time. Not in words, but in action. He went home. We know this because Exodus 4:27 BSB says:

> *Meanwhile, the Lord had said to Aaron, 'Go and meet Moses in the wilderness.' So he went and met Moses at the mountain of God and kissed him.*

The fact that Aaron met Moses at the *'mountain of God'* means that Moses had thrown in the towel, given up and gone home. It was at Sinai that Aaron managed to talk him into going down to Egypt and confronting Pharaoh.

Then, of course, as we know, the ten plagues happened. Let's skip over nine of them to the time just before the tenth plague. Let's go to the first Passover when the Israelites had been told to choose a lamb or a kid and:

> *keep it until the fourteenth day of the month, when the whole assembly of the congregation of Israel will slaughter the animals at twilight. They are to take some of the blood and put it on the sides and tops of the doorframes of the houses where they eat the lambs.*

> Exodus 12:6–7

This is a threshold covenant. Blood is painted on the lintels and the doorposts as a welcome sign. There were no balloons or banners back in those days. When people were anticipating the arrival of an honoured guest, they displayed a symbol of hospitality: blood on the lintels and doorposts that would drip onto the threshold and be caught in a shallow basin carved into the cornerstone. This was a sign the lamb or kid or fatted calf had been slaughtered and was barbecuing out the back. The feast was ready to begin! The celebration was contingent only on the guest accepting the threshold covenant.

The guest signified such acceptance simply by passing over the cornerstone. If he wanted to refuse the offer of hospitality, he would strike the cornerstone instead. All the words in Scripture about *striking* stones, *dashing* feet against stones, *hitting, tripping, trampling* and *stumbling* against stones have the same basic meaning: they refer to *refusing* a covenant, involving hospitality and friendship.

The first Passover, according to Henry Clay Trumbull, was an invitation to God to accept the hospitality of the family and join in a covenantal feast with them. By passing over the stone where the blood had pooled after dripping from the lintels and doorposts, God became a guest at the table and entered into mutual obligation with the host. They were now required to defend each other to the death.

Exodus 12:23 NIV says that God *'will see the blood on the top and sides of the doorframe and will pass over that doorway; so He will not allow the destroyer to enter your houses and strike you down.'*

If you think about this, you will see it can be read in a way that means God has entered the house and become its covenant defender.

Let me carefully differentiate at this moment between a *blood* covenant and a *threshold* covenant. They are not the same. A blood covenant, a divine blood covenant that is, is *all of God*. The obligations are *all* on His side. We don't have to worry about anything. It's up to Him to keep the covenant, not us. Just as Abram was asleep when God raised a blood covenant with Him, so we are asleep, dead in our sins, when God raises a blood covenant with us.[22]

Blood covenant is meant to wake us up. So when it comes to threshold covenant, we should not only be awake but be prepared to uphold mutual obligations. This is where matters can go tragically wrong. Because theologians of the last century have crunched several different covenants basically down to blood contract, we have many erroneous ideas about covenant. One of these is that all the duties and responsibilities of keeping covenant are up to God. But that's not the case with name or threshold covenants, let alone the covenant of salt or covenant of peace.

Now the first Passover went spectacularly well and God defended those households who'd invited Him to dinner against the Angel of Death. The next threshold in this story is the crossing of the Red Sea. Or the Reed Sea. There have been arguments over this for about a century because the Hebrew word is a very interesting one: it looks like *reed*[23], 'suph' but, personally, I think it's so close in spelling to 'saph', *threshold*[24] that that's what it's really meant to evoke. The *Threshold Sea* or *Waters of Transition*.

And just as in the first threshold mentioned in the book of Exodus—the reeds on the banks of the river Nile—contained dangers such as crocodiles, cobras, mambas, vipers, monitor lizards and hippos, so too this threshold on the shore of the Sea contained spiritual dangers that aren't spelled out in the text but are encoded in the description of the landscape. Python was here, the spirit of constriction; Leviathan was here, the spirit of retaliation; Rachab was here, the spirit of wasting; Ziz was here, the spirit of forgetting; and no doubt Azazel and the others were too.[25]

These landscape encodings are confirmed elsewhere in Scripture. Psalm 74:13–14 NIV says,

> *You divided the sea by Your strength; You broke the heads of the sea serpents in the waters. You broke the heads of Leviathan in pieces, and gave him as food to the people inhabiting the wilderness.*

And Isaiah 51:9 NIV says,

> *Was it not You who cut Rahab to pieces, who pierced through the dragon?*

Despite the intense spiritual opposition, despite being hemmed in on every side and facing enemies on every flank, God as covenant defender made a way for the Israelites where there was no way.

This is what a threshold should look like because this is what a threshold covenant with God should mean: total and unassailable defence, an impenetrable shield of protection. The armour of God *should* mean we are covered for every eventuality. It *should* mean being able to walk through the Sea of Transition as if it is dry land, while seeing the barrier that had blocked our way forward heaped up on both sides. This is what it *should* look like.

But for almost all of us the doorway into our calling looks like ground zero of a nuclear explosion. And just a little bit further into the story of Moses we find out why. At the Passover, the families of Israel had invited God to dinner and made a threshold covenant with Him. God had plans to reciprocate when they arrived at Mount Sinai: come to My banqueting hall, He basically said, and celebrate with Me. I want to offer you all, as a nation, not just as families, a threshold covenant. This is the essential thrust of what happens in Exodus 24:9–11 NIV.

> *Then Moses went up, also Aaron, Nadab, and Abihu, and seventy of the elders of Israel, and they saw the God of Israel. And there was under His feet as it were a paved work of sapphire[26] stone, and it was like the very heavens in its clarity. But on the nobles of the children of Israel He did not lay His hand. So they saw God, and they ate and drank.*

This was a really serious event because seventy, as we have seen, is basically the number of world government in Scripture. So God was saying to these seventy men that they were His chosen representatives to bring in a rule of justice, mercy, truth and peace for their own people, and as a model for the entire world.

Because it's threshold covenant, He's promised to defend them as they carry out His command.

But these elders of Israel were no different from Moses. He called them *'stiff-necked'* but he was in fact exactly the same. Just as he covenanted with some idol in that desert shrine on the way to Egypt, they too decided on a similar venture. The sight of God terrified them and they basically informed Moses: 'We're never doing that again. You can have this all to yourself, Moshe. You talk to God from now on, we're happy to take a back-seat.'

So Moses stayed behind and went further up the mountain with God. There he spent forty days while he was being given the Ten Commandments as well as various instructions from God about the design and operation of the Tabernacle.

Finally going down the mountain, he found that Aaron had been presiding over the construction of a golden calf. You couldn't get a more blatant breach of threshold covenant than this. The elders of Israel had been on God's sapphire banqueting floor and they knew exactly what accepting God's hospitality meant. They knew they were required to defend God's name and honour to the death. They knew they should have prevented the construction of the calf instead of aiding and abetting it. But, like Moses stepping into that desert shrine, they perhaps hoped the golden calf would protect them from the consequences of covenant violation.

As I said previously, it's one thing to take a man out of Egypt but entirely another to take Egypt out of the man.

Now when Moses realised what had happened, he called on the people to make good their promise to God. He asked them to take out their swords and defend God's honour by slaying the covenant-breakers. But only the tribe of Levi responded to his summons. This was to have immense consequences for the nation.

Prior to this moment, every male had the right to be priest for his own household and every firstborn son the right to be a priest for the wider family. This entitlement was swept away and, hereafter, only the Levites were permitted to be priests. The reasoning was simple: the people of Israel had demonstrated that they were treacherous and untrustworthy when it came to threshold covenant. Only the Levites had shown a willingness to repent. So now the cornerstone where the blood dripped from the doorposts and which was, in itself, a family altar would be replaced by a threshold within the Tabernacle itself.

This replacement of an altar hearth within the family tent by the mercy-seat on the Ark of the Covenant is demonstrated by its name: *the mercy-seat* is named for the *cornerstone*. Moreover, as we have already seen, Yom Kippur, the Day of Atonement, has a name deriving from mercy-seat and ultimately from cornerstone.

Atonement, *at-one-ment*, the state of being made at one with another person, is the essential nature of covenant. It's not contract, rather it's coming into *oneness* with another.

one in one we are together we are.

Together We are

In blood covenant, God says, 'There is no longer your family and My family. You and I are (one) family.'

In name covenant, God says, 'There is no longer you and Me. It's ("we.") We're friends and we share secrets.'

In threshold covenant, God says, 'There is no longer your business and My business. I have a partnership in mind. You can't fulfil this calling without Me, so we're in it as one. You have absolutely no idea the opposition we're facing. But by the way, I will defend you as My own.'

First, it's about coming into one family, then it's about coming into friendship, then into calling. We can often be persuaded to believe in the theological position that relationship with God happens in a lightning flash, not over a period of years. We look at Moses and we think he fulfilled his calling but in fact he never got there. He only got close. He was called to lead the people into the Promised Land and to take up an inheritance there, not to lead them to the verge and then die on a mountaintop.

Every day for forty years, God sent down 'manna' from heaven. Manna, like the name God wanted to give Moses, means *'what is it?'* Every day God reminded Moses he was being offered a new name. And from time to time, an even more poignant tragedy repeated itself, as described in Exodus 33:7–11 NIV:

> *Now Moses used to take a tent and pitch it outside the camp some distance away, calling it the 'tent of meeting'. Anyone inquiring of the Lord would go to the tent of meeting outside the camp... As Moses*

went into the tent, the pillar of cloud would come down and stay at the entrance, while the Lord spoke with Moses. Whenever the people saw the pillar of cloud standing at the entrance to the tent, they all stood and worshipped, each at the entrance to their tent. The Lord would speak to Moses face to face, as one speaks to a friend.

As one speaks to a friend. God came and came and came again—but He was always on the outside of the tent. You don't leave your friends standing at the door, as Moses did, time after time. God wanted to be Moses' friend and to pass over the threshold into the tent but Moses simply couldn't do it.

As a tiny baby, there was a confusing message about thresholds imprinted on Moses' heart: they are places of abandonment where dangerous and hostile predators roam and where those who love you risk saving your life by leaving you alone in an unpredictable and savage environment.

The tension and the conflict in this messaging[27] where safety is equated with danger and abandonment with love explains a lot about Moses' fears—he can lead his nation into accepting threshold covenant but he can't go there himself.

As I pointed out previously, God compromised. Just as Jesus toned down His question to Simon Peter from 'Do you love Me with a sacrificial agápē love?' to 'Do you love Me like a brother?', then God says to Moses, '*Speak to the rock and draw water from it.*'

This is a gentle reworking of Moses' name, letting him keep the Egyptian essence of it, but still turning it around.

But Moses didn't speak to the rock. He struck it. Now there are all sorts of theological implications to this concerning Christ the Rock, but no one who actually witnessed what Moses did had the slightest idea that he'd just ruined a prophecy. How could they? We can know in retrospect, but the Assembly of the Israelites didn't. What they could have known was that Moses struck a rock. In those days, *striking* a rock meant *refusing* a covenant. It was very public; it was hugely dishonouring. And after over twelve thousand chances, God had had enough. 'That's it,' He said to Moses. 'You can't pass over into the Promised Land.'

When we don't know about threshold covenants, we're tempted to think God's reaction at this point is incredibly snippy, short-tempered and hard to please. After all, Moses might have disobeyed but did it really warrant such an extreme punishment? But what we don't realise is that it isn't a punishment: God gave Moses *exactly* what he asked for. Moses struck the rock, refused covenant and indicated in front of thousands of witness, 'I don't want a name covenant because I don't want to go.' But then, having indicated he didn't want to cross the threshold and pass over the Jordan, he did an astonishing about-face and tried to bargain with God. In Deuteronomy 3:25 NIV, he is reported as saying, *'Please let me go over and see the good land beyond the Jordan, that good hill country and Lebanon.'*

This is a stunning request and its implications aren't particularly clear unless you're aware of the geography. What Moses was asking for was to not *pass over* but to *go around*. He didn't want to cross the Jordan but to go way up north into Lebanon and then to come down into the Promised Land by a coastal route.

A tremendous number of us are like this. We have an instinctive terror of thresholds and we want some way around. It could be something that was imprinted on our hearts at a very early age or it can even be a generational disquiet. But like Moses, we simply can't face our fear of a personal threshold.

I'm one of those people who has been terrified of the threshold. I didn't know that I was; but in retrospect, it's so obvious that was my problem. From time to time now, I catch momentary glimpses of the dreadful majesty of these fallen powers and realise I was right to be scared. But then it dawns on me: God is greater and more majestic still.

So I feel for Moses and the trauma he suffered as a baby. It was so deeply imprinted on his heart that, despite God showing him that He'd part the sea, and despite God's amazing protection throughout the years in the wilderness, Moses could not step up to the cornerstone and do the honouring thing. His inability to overcome this weakness had devastating consequences two generations down the track. This sin, *and it is sin*, became iniquity affecting his bloodline. And it was so serious that his grandson's own reaction to a threshold destroyed everything it took Moses and his brother, Aaron, forty years to build.

Because he rejected God, all Moses was ever allowed to do was look at the Promised Land from a distance. During his lifetime, he never got the inheritance God wanted for him. But what is amazing about His appearance during the Transfiguration is twofold: first, God has allowed him one of his last requests—to go up to the hill country and Lebanon! Yes—gracious, incomprehensibly gracious, is our God! He changed His mind, even though He told Moses not to ask again. Despite Scriptural evidence to the contrary, we often take the theological stance that God never changes His mind—as if His omnipotence and omniscience would thereby be tarnished. However God values relationship so much that He is willing to put us above such things.

The second amazing aspect of Moses talking to Jesus is that he's finally stepped up to a threshold—the Transfiguration, being six days after the name covenant for the church at Caesarea Philippi, is integral to a threshold covenant.

Just as Elijah found it possible to face his greatest fear and stand up in the stronghold of the young lions *because Jesus was there*, so Moses found it possible to step up to the threshold *because Jesus was there*.

If you learn nothing else from this book than *'go with Jesus'*, it's enough. Because, when it comes to rejection, there's a huge takeaway point from that mountaintop meeting: Jesus has set up His church to do better than Moses and better than Elijah, those archetypal heroes of the faith. He is our covenant defender, and He is more than willing to show us how to overcome rejection and live in complete fullness of life.

Scripture is full of stories of ancient people on thresholds making mistakes. When Jesus came down the Mountain of Transfiguration with Cephas, James and John, they all joined up with the remainder of His disciples. Now what had those disciples been doing while the others were away? It's revealed that they'd been attempting to cure an epileptic boy.

> When they came to the crowd, a man came up to Jesus and knelt before Him. 'Lord, have mercy on my son,' he said. 'He has seizures and is suffering terribly. He often falls into the fire or into the water. I brought him to Your disciples, but they could not heal him.'
>
> 'O unbelieving and perverse generation!' Jesus replied. 'How long must I remain with you? How long must I put up with you? Bring the boy here to Me.' Then Jesus rebuked the demon, and it came out of the boy, and he was healed from that moment.
>
> Afterward the disciples came to Jesus privately and asked, 'Why couldn't we drive it out?' '

He answered, 'Because you have so little faith. For truly I tell you, if you have faith the size of a mustard seed, you can say to this mountain,[28] *"Move from here to there," and it will move. Nothing will be impossible for you.'*

Matthew 17:14–20 BSB

Let's recognise what's happening in this scene. Jesus had returned to Caesarea Philippi to gather His disciples. He was about to send them out through the villages of Galilee and Samaria on that governmental mission that, eight centuries previously, Elijah was supposed to have undertaken. However, before He could even mention the assignment He was about to dole out, He was confronted by a father whose son suffered terrible seizures. Now, most people, when they notice Jesus' totally unsympathetic rebuke, *'O unbelieving and perverse generation!'* can't believe He would say it to a desperate father—so they think it's directed at His disciples. No, not at all. Jesus *really* is *really* angry with the father.

Remember what's at Caesarea Philippi? If you answered, 'Gates of Hell' or 'Temple of Pan', you're on the right track as to why Jesus wasn't tempering His words with kindness. After all, there can't be too many reasons why a father brought his epileptic son to the shrine of a goat-demon. In fact, it wasn't necessary for the gospel writers to spell it out for any first century reader. They'd have immediately realised the father was there to offer a sacrifice for his son.

In the time of Jesus, epilepsy was known as 'panolepsy' and was understood to indicate possession by the satyr Pan. So people would go to his temple to make offerings in the hope of release. There's no doubt that's what the father was there for—he'd abandoned faith in Yahweh and was prepared to do whatever the priests of Pan asked of him in order to secure his son's cure.

'O unbelieving and perverse generation!' is the comment of Jesus on the willingness of the father to covenant with the spirit of rejection, of panic, and of unreasoning fear, through a votive offering or sacrifice—a covenant that would affect all his generations henceforth. The man was about to bind himself and his family to the 'scapegoat': Pan of the Greeks, Azazel of the Hebrews.

Millennia before Pan set up a worship centre at Caesarea Philippi, this same area was Azazel's territory. Scripture doesn't give us much detail regarding this fallen entity. It's only mentioned four times, always in Leviticus 16 and always in connection with the ritual for the Day of Atonement:

> *Aaron... must take the two male goats and present them to the Lord at the entrance of the Tabernacle. He is to cast sacred lots to determine which goat will be reserved as an offering to the Lord and which will carry the sins of the people to the wilderness of Azazel. Aaron will then present as a sin offering*

the goat chosen by lot for the Lord. The other goat, the scapegoat chosen by lot to be sent away, will be kept alive, standing before the Lord. When it is sent away to Azazel in the wilderness, the people will be purified and made right with the Lord.

Leviticus 16:6–10 NLT

Later in the same chapter, these instructions are repeated and amplified:

When Aaron has finished performing the ritual to purify the Most Holy Place, the rest of the Tent of the Lord's presence, and the altar, he shall present to the Lord the live goat chosen for Azazel. He shall put both of his hands on the goat's head and confess over it all the evils, sins, and rebellions of the people of Israel, and so transfer them to the goat's head. Then the goat is to be driven off into the desert by someone appointed to do it. The goat will carry all their sins away with him into some uninhabited land... The man who drove the goat into the desert to Azazel must wash his clothes and take a bath before he comes back into camp.

Leviticus 16:20–22;26 GNT

Many English translations do not use the name Azazel at all, instead substituting the invented word, *scapegoat*. As I mentioned previously, many theologians have problems with the notion that God would instruct the high priest to send off an animal chosen by lot into the wilderness to placate a goat-demon. However, as also noted before, their efforts at demythologising this divine direction do not take into account Jesus' visit to the wilderness shrine of a pagan goat-god on the Day of Atonement.[29] The inescapable conclusion from His actions is that Azazel is indeed a fallen cosmic power.

Perhaps the idea that Azazel is not a spiritual entity arises because of later practices regarding the scapegoat. These later practices confuse the issue by converting the scapegoat into a sacrificial animal. However, originally it was simply a carrier of sin—the high priest laid hands on it, transferring all the sins of the people to it and then it was sent off to Azazel to take those sins back where they came from.

A goatherd led the animal a three days' journey into the desert, left it there and hurried back. But, occasionally, a scapegoat would wander back home. And, of course the symbolism associated with any such re-appearance of a sin-laden goat was seriously negative—though less so if the crimson ribbons dangling from its horns had turned white.

> 'Come now, let us reason together,' says the Lord. 'Though your sins are like scarlet, they will be as white as snow; though they are as red as crimson, they will become like wool.'
>
> Isaiah 1:18 ESV

The ribbons were dyed scarlet with an extraction from the scale-insect, *cermes vermilio*, or 'tolah', *worm*, in Hebrew. This scarlet dye naturally turned white in three days when exposed to sunlight, symbolising the Lord's forgiveness and removal of sin. Skeins of identical crimson-dyed ribbon to those tied to the horns of the scapegoat were fixed to the doors of the Temple.

To stop the animal coming home, the priests eventually decided on precautions not specified in Scripture. They instructed the goatherd to throw the goat off a jagged, rocky precipice.[30] This, of course, changed the symbolism: no longer was the goat taking the sins of the people back to where they came from; it was taking them over a cliff. To accommodate this, later traditions about Azazel regard it as dwelling in the desert, chained to jagged rocks.[31]

In these later times, the rabbinic understanding of 'Azazel' thus came to be *precipice*, whereas its original meaning was *entire removal, strength of God* or *she-goat of going away*.

Despite the importance of the scapegoat ritual on the Day of Atonement, Scripture conveys little extra information about Azazel. What is provided is ambiguous and obscure. Jewish tradition gives us a few more clues—yet these must be used with discretion and discernment.

One additional source of information about Azazel is the Book of Enoch. This extra-biblical narrative was extremely popular in first century Galilee and is quoted extensively throughout the epistles and gospels.[32] While the Book of Enoch is not sanctioned as Scripture, it was highly valued by the early followers of Jesus.

Enoch tells us that Azazel was one of the leaders of the Watchers—angels who descended to Mount Hermon and who there pledged[33] to seek out human women and mate with them. Although the chief instigator of this rebellion against God is usually named as Samyaza,[34] it is also said at one point that the overall leader is Azazel. One possible interpretation that resolves this conflict is that Samyaza was the leader earth-side, while Azazel was in command of the traitors while in heaven.

The offspring of the union between these Watchers and human women were the giants of old, the mighty ones who terrorised the earth. When these giants died, their spirits began roaming the world, looking for opportunities to become re-embodied. They craved to be encased in flesh once more—preferably human, but animal would do. These spirits were, in fact, simply demons.

In the time of Jesus, this understanding of the origin of demons prevailed: they were the dead spirits of the offspring of fallen angels and their beautiful human wives.[35] When Jesus started casting them out, great excitement ensued—because there was a significant tradition that one of the identifying signs of the Messiah would be His ability to cast out demons.[36] None of the old-time prophets did this.

At this point, let me sound a note of caution. Demons are *not* fallen angels. They are *not* fallen cosmic powers—rather they are the dead spirits of the hybrid offspring of those powers. Like their angelic fathers, who hungered to mate with human beings, they hunger to be re-united with flesh. In this book, when I use the term 'demonic', I am referring to these Nephilim, *not* to fallen angels. It might seem pedantic to make such a difference, but I'm doing it for a very good reason. Many believers have fallen afoul of threshold guardians and become subject to savage retaliation because they are unaware of the distinction: you don't *bind* fallen cosmic powers, you *ask God to rebuke them.* Back in the first chapter, we noted that Jude and Peter both warn against reviling and dishonouring the forces of the satan. In the Book of Job, God Himself warns against binding Leviathan—and these cosmic spirits belong to the same order as that fearsome seraph-like being. They are threshold guardians.

It is no coincidence that Jesus created the threshold for His church in their territory. When He speaks of the 'kaph', *cornerstone*, and gives Simon the name Cephas, He is not just at Pan's temple. He is also in the shadow of Mount Hermon, just a few minutes' walk from the place where Enoch reportedly ascended to heaven on behalf of the Watchers: 'I went and sat by the waters of Dan in the land of Dan, which is southwest of Hermon.'[37]

According to the Book of Enoch, the angels who descended from heaven with the specific intent of mating with human women came to bitterly regret their action. Their children were monsters, without hope of redemption. Barred from heaven themselves, they sought a righteous human who could present an appeal to God for permission to return. This person was Enoch who was approached by them at the waters of Dan. When he had received God's answer from the heavenly court, he went to deliver it to the Watchers whom he heard 'sitting and weeping at Abel-Maîm, which is between Lebanon and Senir.'[38] Their plea was rejected.

It is perhaps fitting then that Dan eventually became synonymous with rejection of God. The descendants of Moses—yes, Moses!—set up a golden calf there. Commentaries on 2 Chronicles 16:4, Abel-Maîm, *meadow of water,* link the name to Abel-beth-maacah, *meadow of the house of Maacah*, about seven kilometres from Dan. All these places—Dan, the waters of Dan and Abel-Maîm—are in the immediate vicinity of Caesarea Philippi and all are in the shadow of Mount Hermon.

Thus the environment Jesus stepped into on the Day of Atonement was steeped in traditions about a righteous man going into the heavenly court—which is exactly what Jesus did when He ascended the Mount of Assembly for the Transfiguration. The landscape is also saturated with stories about the fall of the angels and about their council chambers on the overshadowing mountain.

The disciples who went there with Jesus would have known the stories about Enoch. And they should have realised that Jesus, *the scapegoat, the worm* and *the cornerstone that was rejected by the builders*, was not there to add his appeal to Enoch's—rather He was there to fulfil the prophecy of Psalm 82 and to announce the end of the reign of the angelic star-shepherds who lorded it over humanity as 'gods of the nations'.

Prayer

Important! Read this first! It is *not* the same preface as in the previous prayer.

The prayers in this book are given as guidelines and jumping-off points for your own interaction with God. I therefore strongly recommend they are read through carefully *before* being prayed aloud with intentionality. If you feel a check in your spirit from the Holy Spirit about any aspect of the prayer, then heed it. Put off praying until you receive permission from God.

It is vitally important to recognise that prayer is about relationship with the Father. None of the words here are intended as a formula and to use them that way is to abuse them. The prayers are nothing in themselves; they are not powerful or guaranteed; they are meant as a start, not as an end in themselves. Power comes from Jesus alone, not from any cleverly—or even wisely—crafted petitions. As a consequence of our intense desire to retain the power we've been gifted and not surrender it back to Jesus, placing it under His authority, these prayers do not use the name Azazel, or Pan, in any declaration of binding or casting out. It is far too easy to fall into the trap of the enemy and become spell-binders through the use of the power of their names, instead of relying on Jesus, the Name above all names, to rebuke the enemy.

Because of the profound importance of *honour* in prayer (discussed in the previous book in the series, *Dealing with Resheph*), each prayer starts with a variation on the theme, 'Hallowed be Your Name'. The shift from dishonour to honour is only possible as we hold onto the hem of Jesus' prayer shawl and ask Him to mediate before the Father for us. In the end, prayer is all about Him!

Father God!—Abba Father! May Your name be kept holy. I ask Jesus, as my mediator, to remove any defilement and dishonour as He presents this prayer to You.

It is written in Your word that You offered a new name to many of our elders in the faith; and since You are the same yesterday, today and tomorrow, I dare to think that You could have a new name for me and I dare to ask what the name unique to me is. What is the name that You have reserved for me from the beginning of time and what is Your unique name that You would reveal to me? O Abba!—draw me deeper into covenantal relationship with You and with Jesus.

O Yahweh! I want to be Your Friend. When my life is over, and You are then still coming soon, I want my headstone engraved to read: 'A Friend of God.' So often You say to me, 'Come on over, and let's lunch together,' and so often in the busyness of life I just keep on hurrying around, absorbed in my own busyness. I don't know how many times I've turned You down. More than Moses? I am crushed to think it might be so.

I repent—I repent for choosing a too busy life that keeps You on the edges and relegates You to the margins. I repent of self-centredness that excludes you and for the pride that accompanies it. I repent of placing myself at the centre of the Universe and rejecting You and Your grace and mercy. I ask Jesus, by His blood, to empower my words of repentance so that my life is transformed.

Yes, Jesus is the Scapegoat but that my sin should make Him so, that I should reject His invitation to friendship, makes me ashamed. I don't want to face that shame, Lord. I want to hide all my shame from You and pretend I have none. That's another lie I need Your help to turn my back on.

I am sorry that I believed lies when all the time You were offering me Truth and a new name and a new covenantal relationship with You. Forgive me, Yahweh. I accept Your forgiveness without reservation, but with humility and friendship. I thank You that my headstone can now be engraved: 'A Friend of God.'

In the name of Jesus, the Chief Cornerstone.

Amen.

3

The Art of War

THERE WAS NO FENCE TO MARK the boundary line between Denis' property and the neighbours'. They were nice enough people with two boisterous boys and a noisy Alsatian. Often the children would chase the dog into Denis' yard during their playtime, terrifying his wife with their excited and unpredictable behaviour. She got to the point where her emotions would spiral into hysterical panic as soon as she even heard the dog barking—regardless of whether it was trespassing or not. And she became hyper-vigilant, always on watch. The moment she saw the boys she would howl at the top of her lungs, sending them running back in fear the way they came. She desperately wanted friends in the neighbourhood but, even after a fence was built, people always avoided her. She couldn't understand why. After all, she'd only ever wanted to feel safe.

She'd never tried to explain to the neighbours the heights of irrational fear she experienced when the dog and the children played in her yard. She was afraid of what they'd think. So, like Pan, she'd used a ghastly scream to defend her 'territory'. Pan was the protecting deity of the countryside—those wild margins beyond the civilised patchwork of cities and towns which, like Denis' property, so often have no clear boundaries. In her anxiety, Denis' wife had called on an ancient technique of rejection while struggling to understand why her behaviour made her neighbours so wary of accepting her. She often felt she was the scapegoat when it came to any conflict in her street.[39]

To understand the agenda of the spirit of rejection, we need to look not only at Pan—and other European variants of this entity—but also at Azazel and Samyaza from the Book of Enoch. It's difficult to distinguish in any certain way between these two at times. On occasion the writer of Enoch called the leader of the Watchers by the name Samyaza[40] but at other times, he was referred to as Azazel.[41] These may be just alternative names for the same entity—Azazel, after all, means *strength of God* and Samyaza means *my name is strength*. And it does make sense for a rebel angel to exclude the theophoric aspect—'*of God*'—from his name.

On the other hand, they may have been separate beings and leadership may have passed from one to the other, as previously indicated, depending on whether they were on earth or in heaven. These angelic insurgents allegedly taught humanity various arcane skills. Azazel passed on the secrets of war—including the making of knives, swords, breastplates and shields—as well as revealing the mysteries of cosmetics, lapidary, and how to devise jewelled ornaments. Samyaza taught the cutting of roots and the occult arts of magical enchantments and spell-binding.[42]

For the purposes of discussing the significance of this forbidden knowledge, I'm going to bundle the teachings of Azazel and Samyaza together. Azazel taught women how to seduce men by beautifying themselves with cosmetics and adorning themselves with jewels. This is, of course, also about 'overcoming' rejection and creating a beguiling counterfeit to God's plan for empowering us against it. He also taught men the art of war, thus providing them with a way of gaining whatever they wanted, regardless of who said 'no' to them. Samyaza basically taught mind control, both by employing the power of words and by using herbal decoctions.

There is nothing intrinsically wrong with the crafting of words,[4] cosmetics, gemstones, metallurgy or herbs— they are great and good gifts of God. However the purposes to which these arts and sciences were bent were defiling and destructive. But the spectacular nature of these skill-and-knowledge sets indicates how easy it would have been for these angels to enthrone themselves as the 'gods of the nations'.

The goat was associated with Greece. The prophet Daniel had a vision in which he was told:

'The shaggy goat is the king of Greece, and the large horn between its eyes is the first king.'

Daniel 8:21 NIV

In Greece, the goat was of course identified with Pan. Now while it's clear to me that Jesus equated Pan and Azazel, it's still worth looking at them more closely to see why, and note what they have in common. For a start, Judd Burton points out that the sound of the Greek word for *goat*, 'aix' (αιξ), is nearly identical to Az and Uz, the Hebrew words for *strength*. He further connects Pan with the Semitic[44] goat deity Uz and points out: 'Uz could mean "goat" or "mountain," and finds a phonetic cousin in Az, and likewise Azazel, who was also associated with the goat, and who descended on to nearby Mount Hermon.'[45]

Apart from their mutual affinity with goats, Pan and Azazel share a lecherous nature. Pan's lust after the nymphs of the fields was as legendary as Azazel's desire for the 'daughters of men'. According to legend, the nymphs were so repelled by Pan's ugliness that they rejected his advances. Greek mythology tells of several incidents when Pan pursued different women, including the story of Syrinx who fled from him and was chased to a riverbank where she begged for help from the water nymphs. They responded by transforming her into reeds. Pan, in frustration, cut the reeds to make the first set of pan pipes, *syrinx*, famed for their evocative, haunting air. The modern word, 'syringe', is derived from *syrinx*.

The Greek name, Pan, originally meant *shepherd*—however, the Romans considered it to derive from the word for *all*. The sense behind the Greek understanding is that Pan was a guardian who watched over his charges. This is evocative of Azazel's position as a leader among the Watchers—those angelic princes who, given rulership of the nations, were seen as 'shepherds' of different people groups.[46] Pan was the 'Good Shepherd' and, as a rustic demi-god, is often considered to be the earliest deity worshipped by the Greeks. When Jesus claimed the title of the 'Good Shepherd', He was not just applying the name to Himself and His Father but implying a stolen designation was being restored to its rightful owners.

Both Pan and Azazel were adept at warcraft: Azazel by teaching metallurgy and weapon-making; Pan by inducing panic. Pan claimed that he had orchestrated the victory in two notable battles: that of the Titans against the gods of Olympus, and that of the Persians against the Athenians. He insisted that his wild cries had so terrorised the Titans, they had faltered in fear; and similarly his howling screams had so panicked the Persians that they lost the Battle of Marathon.

Both Azazel and Pan were worshipped in deserted places. Azazel was a spirit of the wilderness and Pan was a godling of the wild, particularly of mountain wastes. The word *pagan*, which originally meant simply *a person who lived in the countryside, beyond the civilising influence of a city,* is sometimes considered to derive from the name of Pan. There's some doubt about this but, on the other hand, the word *panic* unquestionably comes from Pan. The pursuit of Pan has worldwide counterparts in many mythologies and folkloric legends as a 'Wild Hunt'—a terrifying chase with violent and haunting spiritual overtones.[47]

Pan was associated with divination and prophecy—however let's clarify that by noting this is 'prophecy' in the old Greek sense of *foretelling*, not the Hebrew sense of *forth-telling*. And while divination is not known as one of the gifts of Azazel—though some modern practitioners of the occult claim their personal experience is otherwise—it may be that the landscape around Caesarea Philippi recorded this connection. Besides the Temple to Pan with its Gates of Hell, there were also shrines to Baal Gad and Baal Aliyan.[48]

Baal Gad was the so-called *lord of fortune*, but fortune was often linked to the casting of 'lots' or a lottery: precisely the method used to choose the scapegoat to be sent out to Azazel. Besides meaning *fortune*, Gad also meant *troops*—naturally associated with war, a specialty of both Azazel and Pan—and it rhymed with 'gedi', *young goat*.[49]

Baal Aliyan was a godling of fountains, flowers and fertility. The son[50] of Baal Hadad, the storm deity opposed by Elijah, Aliyan's name is thought to mean *strong* and to be cognate with Uzzah, Uz and Az—once more evoking Azazel.

In summary, both Pan and Azazel were divinities associated with goats and the wilderness. Both pursued women and renowned for their lusts. Both were watchers and shepherds. Both were involved with warcraft. Both were amongst the oldest and earliest 'rulers of the nations'. Jesus effectively identified them as equivalent in function, if not in name, when He went to the Gates of Hell in Caesarea Philippi on Yom Kippur. By inaugurating His church at this time and in this place, He was declaring war on those who taught war to mankind. He followed up this proclamation by standing, six days later, in their war council on the Mount of Assembly. He took with Him the two most famous prophets in the entire history of the Israelite people. These men had experienced such unreasoning, unresolvable fear for so long that their reaction to it had affected the destiny of the nation they were shepherding. Neither of them during their time on earth had truly overcome the spirit of panic—except in limited ways.

But now, with Jesus beside them, they could conquer that fear and the sense of rejection allied with it.

They could do just what God had told Cain to do: *master it.*

The *wasting*, the natural consequence of failing to prevail over rejection, was now in Jesus' hands.

After God confronted me with the question, 'And just why would you want to teach anyone to handle rejection?', I set about re-assessing everything I did.

When I considered the matter objectively, I realised I just ignored rejection. That was my way of 'handling' it.

My dad had mastered the technique of rejecting others before they rejected him; my mother froze into silence; one of my brothers, in his own words, 'built a bridge and got over it'. But I just pretended it didn't exist. When it involved the rejection of a manuscript I'd submitted to a publishing company, I could stave off the feelings of discouragement with a coffee or a good, long session of 'sits and thinks'. When it involved personal rejection, I'd head off to my girl-cave for a while and read a book to distract myself.

Not exactly *triumphing* over rejection, when it came right down to it. In fact, exactly like heading into a false refuge. It didn't take more than half a second to realise the hunt of Pan is a spiritual strategy to drive us straight to the special sanctuary we've created for ourselves— our instinctive hiding place in times of trouble. That safe shelter we've stocked with creature comforts to console us.

The spirit of rejection wants us to choose a haven that is a counterfeit of heaven. A truly pitiful counterfeit, when we examine it. As I testified in *Hidden in the Cleft: True and False Refuge*,[51] it took me decades to understand my ever-present help in time of trouble was not God but a cup of coffee. Sure, I eventually got around to talking to God—but my first port of call when I was crushed or disappointed was a long, strong coffee.

As soon as I realised I had created a false refuge out of habitual 'ignoring', I first repented of it, then had several long chats to God. I also asked my friends to have a chat with Him themselves and see what He told them.

One had had an image of *red hair*.

The other spoke about *atonement*.

I got the verse from Malachi, *'Jacob I loved but Esau I hated.'*

Back twenty years ago, I might have dismissed all of these answers as vain imaginings. I've learned better over time. I've discovered that, if God is handing out jigsaw pieces, then it's wise to keep talking to Him until He provides an understanding of how they fit together. In this case, it took nearly two weeks of chatting with Him before I realised that all these messages, as strange and disparate as they seemed, were profoundly interconnected.

Sure, any red-headed individual, especially in days gone by, is an expert when it comes to rejection experiences. But that was not the message about *red hair*. The significance of the symbol and its relation to the other messages only came to the fore when I thought of separating the words *red* and *hair*. Both words, in Hebrew, point to Jacob's twin brother, Esau, who went by two other names: Edom meaning *red* and Seir meaning *hairy*.

However, Seir is also a word for *goat*. This immediately connects it with the scapegoat of the Day of Atonement. And, as I considered the matter, I recognised that the ultimate rejection symbol is the scapegoat.

So I started investigating Azazel and collected the research I've presented so far in this book. I realised Jesus had symbolised Himself as the scapegoat by going to a goat-demon's shrine and standing in front of the Gates of Hell on the Day of Atonement in the year before He died. At that time, He'd spoken His church into being and, in Hebrew, He'd used the word for *cornerstone*. But as we know, this is a rejected cornerstone because Jesus is the stone that was tossed aside by the builders but still became the head of the corner. (Psalm 118:22; 1 Peter 2:7; Mark 12:10; Acts 4:11; Matthew 21:42; Luke 20:17)

The threshold of the church is the Cornerstone that was rejected. Rejection is built into the very foundation of our existence as Christ's Body.

At first sight, this is absolutely the worst possible news for those of us wanting to be rid of rejection. Is it possible to eliminate something so intrinsic to our called-out nature?

While pondering the thought that perhaps God commanded us to *master* rejection because it was impossible to eliminate it, I realised the gospels tell us that six days[52] after this event, Jesus went up a high mountain, was transfigured in glory and heard the approving words of the Father: *'This is My beloved Son, My Chosen One.'*[53]

Wait! That wasn't rejection! What more acceptance could you want in life than to hear similar words directly from God? So I developed a theory and I said to my friends who were asking for help: 'I've got it all sussed out. At least I think I have. Sit with Jesus as the rejected cornerstone for six days and you get to the place of being the beloved.'

I decided to be my own guinea-pig for the experiment. If my theory was correct, it would only take six days. And all I had to do was, whenever I felt even the slightest hint of rejection or panic, go to Jesus and be in His presence as I *experienced* it.

So for six days I sat with Jesus in rejection… and another six days… and another six. I was beginning to have serious doubts about my theory and I said to God, 'This is taking a lot longer than I expected.'

He said to me: 'That's because you keep dropping out of the place of rejection. You're defaulting back into handling mode.'

Really? I was surprised. 'I wasn't aware I was doing that.'

'You've mastered the art of ignoring rejection,' God said to me. 'Let me ask you: how many times have you been rejected in life?'

I thought for a moment but nothing sprang to mind. 'Not often,' I said. 'Nothing like other people. I'm very fortunate in that respect.'

There was a short pause. Perhaps God had dropped His head into His hands, wondering which incident to bring up first. 'What about the time you were expecting to announce your engagement and your fiancé got up and announced it to someone else? Wasn't that rejection?'

I felt the quick flicker of a stab wound to the heart but brushed it aside. 'Oh, yeah. I'd forgotten about that.'

'And what about the time that your best and only friend at high school simply stopped talking to you and never ever came near you again? Wasn't that rejection?'

I had never found out why she did that. We'd lived in each other's pockets for nearly five years until, one day, without a word of explanation she took up with some other girls. 'I'd forgotten about that too,' I told God.

He wasn't finished. 'And what about the time all your friends in that social club treated you like slime because of something one of them said about you? Something that none of them has ever been willing to reveal or ask you if it were true or not? Isn't that rejection?'

I took a deep breath as I recalled the time more than twenty people turned their backs on me and just walked away as if I had the plague. I never did find out what had been said. For years, I was desperate to learn what it was—until one day I realised God was asking me to surrender my need to know. For someone whose life revolves around the word, 'Why?' that was an incredibly hard ask.

I suddenly recognised, in the light of God's questions, that I did the same thing as one of my brothers when it came to rejection. I built a bridge and I got over it.

Trouble was, I'd never thought much of his way of dealing with things. Building a bridge wasn't really forgiving—it was ignoring.

God was still bringing up the past. He went on and on, reminding me of the times I'd been sidelined for standing up for others or standing up for myself. There were incidents so painful it had taken years to properly forgive the people involved. I'd think I had, but then some trigger would come up, and I'd have to forgive them all over again.

How on earth had I forgotten all this stuff? It was raw; and the rejection hurt in a way that it shouldn't. 'Have I not truly forgiven these people?' I asked God.

'There are many things you've forgiven them for,' God said. 'But not for their cooperation with rejection.'

Cooperation with rejection? I had a very, very, very bad feeling about all this. It dawned on me—eventually— that the three apostles who'd headed up the Mount of Transfiguration were the same three who'd been present in the Garden of Gethsemane. I said to God, 'Overcoming rejection is going to be like staying in Gethsemane with Jesus, isn't it? It's going to really, really hurt. It's going to be seriously unpleasant, right? I don't think I can do it. I need help.'

Even knowing it was for only six days, I didn't believe I could make it through. If the disciples couldn't watch one hour, how was I going to make it through almost a whole week? I'd already tried it and discovered I could default to my false refuge without even knowing it.[54]

But God is immeasurably faithful. He helped me to cease ignoring rejection. He helped me to sit in it with Jesus the rejected cornerstone. He helped me to stop turning my back on rejection and on the presence of Jesus at the same time. He helped me endure the sadness, the panic, the sense of being hunted and—worst of all—the knowledge that, if they had their time over, the same people would reject me in the same way once again. And they wouldn't explain their actions this time either. Everything would be just as baffling and inexplicable as it had always been.

So I sat with Jesus the rejected cornerstone.

One day passed.

Two days passed.

Then three days.

Four days.

On the fourth day, I noticed that the spirit of rejection had done a bunk. Things were much clearer. It was as if a veil had lifted. 'Why, look at that…' I said to Jesus. 'Now that the spirit of rejection has gone, I can see there was something hiding behind it.'

I looked closer and, suddenly, I recognised what I was seeing and feeling within my own spirit. Multitudes—I mean, *multitudes*—of swearwords sprang to my lips.

I had discerned a spirit of wishing.

It's an understatement to say I was devastated. I thought I'd got rid of the wishmaiden nearly two decades previously. As a child, a snare had been laid for me by a spirit-being best described as an oskmær, a *wishmaiden*, and I had trapped it at the very moment it trapped me. In *Dealing with Resheph*, I tell the story of how a forgotten trauma shaped my life.[55]

But seriously—had I been entirely mistaken that this entity had gone? How had I missed noticing its presence? I'd been so careful to keep all known doors of access shut: I kept clear of any symbols of wishing—that wasn't particularly hard since I'd always felt uneasy around them and studiously tried to avoid them. Apparently it had snuck back into my life and hidden itself in the fog that swirled around the spirit of rejection.

Thinking about what I'd 'seen'—a spirit-woman sitting in a nest in the sea—it reminded me of the description of the Whore of Babylon. As the angel reveals to John about his vision:

> *The waters you saw, where the prostitute sits, are peoples, multitudes, nations and languages.*

> Revelation 17:15 NIV

Reading the wider context, it sounded to me like this woman was a trader in souls. Obviously she was in the same line of business as the satan who, according to Ezekiel 28:16, was an anointed cherub cast out of heaven for trading. I believe that the Hebrew of this passage indicates he was trading in names—that is, in identities, destinies, callings and, by extension, souls.[56] One of the Hebrew words for *soul*, after all, contains the word for *name*.

Also in Ezekiel, the trading of souls is linked to soul-hunters:

> *Woe to the women who sew magic bands upon all wrists, and make veils for the heads of persons of every stature, in the hunt for souls! Will you hunt down souls belonging to my people and keep your own souls alive?*

Ezekiel 13:18 ESV

The magic bands on wrists and heads[57] are clearly counterfeits of phylacteries and prayer tassels—those divinely ordained wearable reminders of God's love and protection. These devices are to assist us with remembering, not forgetting. By creating arcane mimics of these holy gifts, occult practitioners not only assist us to forget, they set in motion their own chilling purpose: to trade any souls they capture and give them over to Death in exchange for their own lives.

In other words: all this was a variation on a covenant with Death.

God prompted me to go and have a look at the meaning of the word 'oskmær'. I got the sense that, twenty years down the track, I'd find more information than I had in pre-Google days. That proved to be right: 'oskmær' was not just *wishmaiden* but *adopted daughter* or *chosen one, the beloved*.

Well, that explained just about everything. No wonder, as I sat with Jesus in rejection—waiting for an announcement from God on the sixth day that I was His beloved adopted daughter, His chosen—it is was necessary for Him to show me the wishmaiden. Everything about it was a hindrance because it indicated a satanic covenant was still operational in my life. If that counterfeit covenant remained, it would undermine the work of overcoming rejection and totally negate God's acceptance of me.

As soon as I realised what the real problem was, I went back to my friends and told them what I'd discovered. At that point, I wasn't sure whether wishing was a problem unique to me or if it was more widespread. They immediately ticked off wishing as a major issue—though other people, subsequently, have not.

Wishing sounds like harmless kid's stuff—'Blow out the candles and make a wish,' 'Wish upon a shooting star,' 'Throw a coin in the fountain and make a wish,' 'Wish me luck,' 'Don't you just wish!'

Wishes can indeed be quite harmless. Yet they can also be immensely dangerous. When we make a wish at a moment of rejection, we step across a dark frontier. At that traumatic instant, we should reach for a prayer, not a wish. We should put our prayer to Jesus and hold onto Him as He stands before the Father; not fling out a wish that may well bring us into deeper agreement with the powers of darkness.

Soul-hunters—whether they are high-level cosmic powers like Pan or humans tormented by fear of losing their own lives and practising witchcraft to avoid it— have a common purpose in wanting to trap us into a wish. We've been herded into a false refuge and thus into a covenant with an entity other than the God and Father of our Lord Jesus Christ.

Who is it we want to empower our words? Jesus, through holding on to the hem of His garment—the tassels of His prayer shawl—as He mediates for us before the Father? Or an unholy spirit through a wish?

It's no coincidence that basic level witchcraft is called wishcraft. Nor is it any coincidence that, in the nineteenth century, the countryfolk of Britain still knew the highest levels of black magic were virtually indistinguishable from prayer. Unless we learn to discern the difference, we remain complicit with rejection's right to always rule over us.

It's a war. Pan and Azazel are both experts at it. Their counterparts in other cultures were often associated with it too: Odin, the chief of the Norse pantheon, was a wargod as well as the leader of the *oskoreia*, the soul-raving Wild Hunt of Scandinavia. He was also the master of the oskmær, the wishmaidens who, like the valkyries, choose heroes for Odin's endtime army.

As soon as I saw in my mind's eye the image of the wishmaiden nesting on the water, I realised how deep my problem was. I've got training in prayer ministry and a great deal of experience in it, but I immediately knew this issue was way above my pay-grade. I could sense that the flotation device the wishmaiden was using was a *mare's nest*. The original meaning of *mare* in this context belongs to nightmare and refers to a 'mara', an Anglo-Saxon and Old Norse term for a demon that sat on sleepers' chests, causing them to have terrifying dreams.[58] Since my childhood nightmares were instigated by an oskmær, I am more than tempted to think 'mara' and 'mær' are related words.

I could instinctively tell what the mare's nest was made of—a snarled tangle of half-finished wishes; dense knots of irrational decisions twisted together by panic; sticky shreds of rejection that had been tossed aside and ignored. There they all were—one gigantic messy roost that was growing bigger by the day. I didn't even know where to start to fix it, let alone how. I surrendered the whole toxic tangle to Jesus with just the simple prayer, 'Help!'

Normally I'd have applied all I knew about sanctification and transformation: I'd have been repenting, confessing, forgiving and renouncing. However, in this instance, it was such an impossible chaotic disaster, I had no clue what to do. So I decided to let Jesus sort it all out for me without my help.

He must have been doing a great job behind the scenes because, about two weeks after I surrendered it all to Him, the biggest temptation about wishing I've ever faced in my entire life occurred. It was unexpected, but the very enormity of it put me on guard. I reiterated that the situation was entirely in the hands of Jesus but I realised I needed specialised help in discernment. I said to God, 'I know You want to give me the desires of my heart but where the desire of my heart ends and a wish begins, I've no idea.'

Several weeks later, I felt Jesus had cleaned up enough for me to begin co-labouring with Him. I was thinking of 1 Corinthians 3:9 ISV: *'we are God's co-workers.'* It was time, I felt, to speak out some repentance I wasn't able to broach at the beginning. 'I know You don't need my help with the atonement, Jesus, and I don't wish to add anything to what You've done or are doing. But I wish to record that I repent of wishing. It's irrelevant what I wished, it's only relevant that I wished. So I wish it to be recorded in heaven that I repent of doing that. I also wish to record my thankfulness to You, Father, for protecting me all these years, despite this alliance with an ungodly spirit. And I wish to record my thankfulness to Jesus for making it possible through His blood to overcome this spirit. And I wish to record...'

For several minutes I went on in this vein until, in a sudden stunned realisation, I clapped my hand over my mouth. I *wish!?*

Everything I was saying started with the words, 'I *wish!*' I hadn't ever prayed like this at any time in my life before. I'd never previously said, 'I wish to record my repentance,' just, 'I repent... and I ask Jesus to empower my words of repentance.'

So I started all over again. 'I repent of wishing. It's irrelevant *what* I wished, it's only relevant *that* I wished. I repent of doing that.'

When I finished, I realised how much scum Jesus was expelling to the surface. It had been so unimaginably deep it took another few months to work through. And when it was all over, Jesus invited me to finish the last two days of the six-day assignment of sitting in His presence.

And when it was over, something unexpected happened. I, of course, had been counting on—well, not an audible Voice emanating from a shining cloud and proclaiming, 'This is My daughter, My beloved, My adopted child, My chosen one!'—but some sense of a similar sentiment arising in my heart.

But no. Instead God said, 'I've got a project for the next forty days I'd like you to be part of.'

'Yes?' I asked warily. Forty days. *Forty:* a number evocative of testing, trials, wilderness experiences.

'Let's get rid of the spirit of wasting in your life.'

'Oh, *yesyesyesyesyes!*' I couldn't think of anything I'd like more.

'It's going to mean *war.*'

'Goes without saying, doesn't it?'

'I'm not talking about spiritual conflict. I mean the Angel.'

'Oh.' I paused to consider the Angel who carried the name War. Suddenly it made perfect sense why I'd never overcome the spirit of wasting. Unless rejection was mastered first, War could not come to my aid.

Prayer

Father God, may Your name be honoured now and always. Lord, time and time again I have been paralysed by fear and panic. I've been rendered useless—immobilised and unable to respond. At other times I've run. At times I've fought, sometimes with defensive words, sometimes with flattery. My destiny and the future of my family have been at risk because I succumbed and surrendered to the effects of fear.

I confess that I am just like Elijah and Moses. I can't conquer my fear unless Jesus is by my side. Like Moses, I am scared of the threshold and, like Elijah, I'm terrified of the enemy hosts ranged against me. Like the father of the boy who wanted his son healed, my heart is perversely in agreement with the spirit of rejection and the spirit of wishing. Instead of reaching for the hand of Jesus to heal my wounds, I've run to my false refuge and, instead of a prayer, I've flung a wish behind me to distract the hunter pursuing me.

I repent of using coping strategies instead of turning straight to Jesus as my shield and my strength. I repent of using wishes and formulae in times of trouble, instead of sitting with Jesus and talking my difficulties through with Him. Father, with Him by my side I am able to do just as You told Cain to do in Genesis: '*Master* it. Do not allow this spirit of fear, panic and rejection to control you, your life and your destiny. *Master it.*'

Father, I cannot subdue any of these spirits in my own strength. There are so many Watchers allied with Azazel that are intent on ensuring I fail. Yet I am called to be a 'watcher' too—but in an entirely different sense. I am called to sit and watch with Jesus as if we are together in the 'oil-press' of Gethsemane. I am called to accept the empowerment He offers. With Him to guide me, I can control these spirits in His name and through the blessing of His blood and the cross. I ask Him, as the Chief Cornerstone to energise my words of repentance, so that they achieve the self-control and the mastery of rejection that You have told us to display on the threshold.

Father, I am truly sorry and repent of a life that has been wasted in so many ways. In Jesus' name I ask You to forgive me, help me identify and crush my false refuges, bury my idols and align my heart with Yours. Annul any covenant I have with the spirit of rejection, and help my unbelief so that I can truly accept the fullness of the atoning death of Jesus.

Holy Spirit, come with Your pure and refreshing water and wash me clean of all traces of fear, panic and rejection. Cleanse deep into the places of trauma where the memory of rejection is lodged and pour healing balm over the memories. Allow me to remember, but without trauma—and, in remembering, help me renounce any agreements with the spirit of forgetting that render me unable to repent or forgive. Make me a vessel fit for the Master's use.

Lord Jesus, embolden and strengthen me to live in the freedom and fullness of life You promise. I ask You, Jesus of Nazareth, to be my mediator and present these petitions to Your Father and mine. I ask that You cleanse them of any and all defilement, dishonour or disrespect that is hidden in my heart and that would hinder the granting of this prayer.

Thank You, Father God.

Thank You, Holy Spirit.

Thank You, Jesus.

In the name of the Chief Cornerstone. Amen.

4

The Art of Corps

'Safe?' said Mr. Beaver, 'don't you hear what Mrs. Beaver tells you? Who said anything about safe? 'Course <u>he isn't safe. But he's good. He's the King, I tell you.'</u>

C.S. Lewis,
The Lion, the Witch and the Wardrobe

I'M WRITING THIS CHAPTER in the last week of the year of fear, 2020. If we've learned anything in this year when the world became obsessed with a 'pandemic' and with a 'vaccine' solution,[59] it's this: <u>many people, not all but a majority, are willing to give up basic human rights to</u> *feel* 'safe'. Not to *be* safe, but to *feel* it.

Politicians throughout the world have trampled on the constitutions of their countries and laws of their states, assuming emergency powers so that their populations would be 'safe'. Listen to the news and the message is fear-fear-fear. Just a few days ago, someone said to me about the lockdown (isn't it interesting how we've co-opted the language of the prison system?) in England over Christmas, 'Two percent of people in London are thought to be infected with coronavirus. Isn't that terrifying?' The thought that 98% of the residents *didn't* have the virus apparently hadn't penetrated the thinking of this man who was genuinely scared for his children living overseas.

The problem with fear is this: lack of it won't protect you, but its presence is like a magnet. If you dismiss fear and indulge in risk-taking behaviour, the dangers are not lessened by your brave front. However if you engage with fear, then as Job recounted:

> *What I fear comes upon me, and what I dread befalls me.*

> Job 3:25 NASB

The twenty-first century's obsession with 'safe' is not a new phenomenon. We can look back on the story of Elijah and see that, like so many of us, he craved 'safe'. The panicked flight to Horeb was an escape to safety. His defiance of God in failing to anoint Jehu or Hazael comes down to a desire for the relative safety and familiarity of Ahab's reign compared to the likely brutality of Jehu's.

Yet behind that longing for security is a distrust of God as a safe refuge. Until that conversation with Jesus on the top of Mount Hermon during the Transfiguration—in the presence of all the enemies Elijah was so terrified of—it's clear that God wasn't enough. Isn't that true for us as well? We want Jesus PLUS a safe refuge, we're not content with Jesus AS a safe refuge.

None of this walking with Jesus our covenant defender through dangerous territory for us; we'd much rather avoid the perilous places altogether. However, we still want to reserve the right to whistle up Jesus for help whenever we find out our armour is dented or we've got stuck in some unexpected quicksand.

We want a safe God and a tame Jesus and a comfortable bypass to any arenas of danger in life. Well, maybe not always. Maybe occasionally we want excitement, even genuine adrenaline-pumping risk—but we don't want any life-altering destructive consequences flowing from those risks. We want God to save us from ourselves—but only *when* we want to be saved from ourselves, not otherwise.

We don't want a God whose goodness and holiness are threats to our safety.

Back at the end of the last chapter, did you think to yourself: *an angel who carries the name War? What? That's not in the Bible! Is it?*

I have to admit that it's not in any English translation. But it's there in the Hebrew and it is a profoundly important Angel when it comes to the spirit of rejection. It's possibly even more important when it comes to the spirit of wasting. This Angel is not only a bearer of the name War, it carries it because God put *His own name* on it.

I can't begin to describe my dismay on realising this. I dislike conflict so intensely that, when anyone mentioned the Armour of God, I'd mentally start looking for a hiding place. Battle? Not for me! Find me a foxhole and find it two minutes ago!

But then I discovered that we receive the Armour of God through His loving kiss—and I was so thrilled. Our paraclete—our battle companion—girds us for battle through a kiss. Taking His love into battle entirely turned my thinking around.

I didn't really understand how unbalanced my thinking had subsequently become until I was reading a commentary on this passage from Exodus:

> *He took the Book of the Covenant and read it to the people. They responded, 'We will do everything the Lord has said; we will obey.'*
>
> *Moses then took the blood, sprinkled it on the people and said, 'This is the blood of the covenant that the Lord has made with you in accordance with all these words.'*
>
> *Moses and Aaron, Nadab and Abihu, and the seventy elders of Israel went up and saw the God of Israel. Under His feet was something like a pavement made of lapis lazuli, as bright blue as the sky. But God did not raise His hand against these leaders of the Israelites; they saw God, and they ate and drank.*

Exodus 24:7–11 NIV

Now Moses sprinkled the blood as part of a covenant rite. *Hmm*, I thought. *But what kind of covenant? It could be blood, but that's hardly likely. Is there any evidence that it's name or threshold or salt or peace?*

The banquet of the seventy elders with God suggested it was a threshold covenant and, as I read on, I found five verses later: *'The glory of the Lord settled on Mount Sinai. For six days the cloud covered the mountain, and on the seventh day the Lord called to Moses from within the cloud.'* The specific mention of *'six days'* was confirmation for me that it was indeed a threshold covenant—but this presented a difficulty. My understanding of the covenantal sequence is that a name covenant should occur six days before a threshold covenant.[60] So I needed to be looking for a name covenant as well.

Back in the previous chapter, God lays out His covenantal conditions in a speech that is a precursor to Moses sprinkling blood on the people. In this extended scene, the word *name* appears. At first sight, it doesn't seem particularly promising, but read carefully:

'See, I am sending an angel ahead of you to guard you along the way and to bring you to the place I have prepared. Pay attention to him and listen to what he says. Do not rebel against him; he will not forgive your rebellion, since **My Name** *is in him. If you listen carefully to what he says and do all that I say, I will be an enemy to your enemies and will oppose those who oppose you. My angel will go ahead of you and bring you into the land of the*

Amorites, Hittites, Perizzites, Canaanites, Hivites and Jebusites, and I will wipe them out. Do not bow down before their gods or worship them or follow their practices. You must demolish them and break their sacred stones to pieces. Worship the Lord your God, and His blessing will be on your food and water. I will take away sickness from among you, and none will miscarry or be barren in your land. I will give you a full life span.

'I will send My terror ahead of you and throw into confusion every nation you encounter. I will make all your enemies turn their backs and run. I will send the hornet ahead of you to drive the Hivites, Canaanites and Hittites out of your way. But I will not drive them out in a single year, because the land would become desolate and the wild animals too numerous for you. Little by little I will drive them out before you, until you have increased enough to take possession of the land.'

Exodus 23:20–30 NIV

The vast majority of English literal translations render Exodus 23:21 as '*My Name is **in him***' though one has the equally valid *within him* and another *with him*. However, the Hebrew word for *in him* happens to be identical to the word for *war*. And as we read this entire passage, it is clear that *war* makes total sense. '*The Lord is a man of war; the Lord is his name,*' sang Moses after the crossing of the Sea of Transition. (Exodus 15:3 ESV)

But if you look closely at the passage from Exodus 23, you'll see that God doesn't just call the Angel by the name *War*, He also calls it *'My terror'* and *'the hornet'*. This is God's answer to Pan and Azazel: yes, they have schemes of war and a panic-inducing battle-disrupting agenda, but God has the Angel He calls His Terror to deploy on behalf of His children.

All angels are scary—their usual greeting is: 'Do not be afraid.' But this Angel is super-scary. It apparently has one function: to go to war. Nothing else. This Angel is tasked with driving out your enemies—and, as any good battle commander does, he will devise a strategy. Our part is to obey orders and fulfil our part in this strategy. So, if we obey him, he battles on our behalf. But, because his only role is war, if we disobey him, he battles against us.

If you cannot face the spirit of rejection and panic, neither can you face the Angel called Terror for long enough to hear its commands and obey them. You'll run, just as you did when panic roared at you. Maybe, hiding in that false refuge you've constructed, you'll come up with a good idea about how this kind of warfare should be conducted. But a good idea is not always a God-idea. As David found when He decided the Ark of the Covenant should be brought to Jerusalem:

> *David... and all his troops set out... to bring up from there the ark of God, which is called by the Name— the name of the Lord of Hosts, who is enthroned between the cherubim that are on it.*

They set the ark of God on a new cart... Uzzah and Ahio, the sons of Abinadab, were guiding the new cart, bringing with it the ark of God...

When they came to the threshing floor of Nacon, Uzzah reached out and took hold of the ark of God, because the oxen had stumbled. And the anger of the Lord burned against Uzzah, and God struck him down on the spot for his irreverence, and he died there beside the ark of God.

2 Samuel 6:2 ESV

Uzzah had the best of intentions. It apparently wasn't even his fault that the Ark was on a cart. He was merely doing what the king wanted. In today's church, we don't want to know about a God who killed an innocent man for inadvertent dishonour. If anyone's to blame, isn't it David? (And while we're playing an accountability game, doesn't Elijah have to share in the responsibility for Naboth's death because he put off anointing Jehu until the never-never?)

Thresholds are incredibly dangerous places—and we have largely forgotten that they are, except when our instincts kick in and fear overwhelms us. However, ancient people were aware of the hazards. They knew they needed a covenant defender for protection. So, while Uzzah meant no disrespect, he still touched a threshold that has no peer: the boundary between heaven and earth guarded by the sword-wielding cherubim. That's what the Ark of the Covenant is: the brink of heaven.

There is only one covenant defender who can guard us from the dangers of Uzzah's namesake, Azazel, as well as from the hazards of the threshold—and it's Jesus. Moses and Elijah both found unparalleled protection in His company as He stood up with them in the Divine Council.

His mere presence and the ringing words of the Father, proclaiming Him as the beloved Son, were a declaration of war against the seventy young lions. By forgetting the prophetic background to His stand, we miss these nuances—Jesus was beginning a process of bringing down a world government. We overlook these allusions, even though He'd just created His ekklesia, usually translated *church* but probably better translated *parliament*,[61] just six days previously.

Yes, six. Like I said: the standard time differential between a name covenant and a threshold covenant.

Jesus not only came to fulfil the Law and its legal requirements—He came to fulfil the unwritten laws of the realm of the heavens and the underworld. Perhaps 'unwritten' is not the correct word because we can find many clues about them in many ancient stories; and perhaps 'laws' is not quite right either. Perhaps 'uncodified principles' is a better, closer description but even that fails to convey the subtle legal nature of these spiritual rules.

Much as I dislike some of the overtones of the word, 'chivalry' possibly suggests how best we are to approach this war. We have to be honourable: to everyone, without exception. Without question, the most common wounding—even fatality—in the war against these cosmic powers is a direct result of hurling abuse at them and then failing to repent of that dishonour.

A war needs weapons.

If you've read the other books in this series, you'll know that God has given us specialised armaments that are specifically designed to take down each of the threshold guardians. Not collectively, but separately. *Love* is what brings down Python,[62] the spirit of constriction; *joy* is what immobilises Ziz, the spirit of forgetting; *peace*— or more accurately 'shalom'—is what eliminates Leviathan-Resheph, the multi-faced spirit that retaliates against dishonour.

Love, joy, peace—if you thought you spotted the beginning of the list describing the Fruit of the Spirit, you'd be absolutely correct. The Fruit of the Spirit are 'weapons' against the threshold guardians.

There's a very simple reason why. In the Garden of Eden, fruit was weaponised against humanity. Because of the spiritual law embedded into the fabric of the universe—*we reap what we sow*—weaponised fruit has naturally turned against its original users and become just as deadly.

Jesus has given us the Fruit of the Spirit to ward off the threshold guardians. So which Fruit overcomes the spirit of rejection?

It's *self-control*, the last of the list.

Now don't fall for the thought that self-control means we have to discipline ourselves through a diligent exercise of our own willpower. Any idea that it's a grit-your-teeth-and-set-your-mind-to-overcoming mode is doomed to failure. As Cain found when God told him to subdue the sin crouching at his door, self-mastery is just not that simple.

The Greek word usually translated *self-control, self-restraint* or *temperance* is 'egkráteia' and the true sense of it is akin to *empowerment.*

Ian contacted me through Facebook because he had a problem with rage. He'd tried everything in his power to forgive and repent and he'd concluded, on reading Scripture, that he needed to persevere in order to be able to control his anger when it exploded without warning. He figured that, at most, he'd have to repent and forgive 490 times—seventy times seven—before it would all be over. To keep track of his progress, he decided he'd paint a leaf every time he repented and forgave.

By the time he contacted me he had over a thousand paintings and he knew something was seriously wrong. However he also had a suspicion from reading a Facebook comment what it might be. So he asked me what I meant by 'asking Jesus to empower your words of repentance.'

Now personally I think that the concept of asking Jesus to empower our words of repentance—and forgiveness, for that matter—is self-evident. He is our mediator, our go-between, our conciliator, the one who presents our prayers to the Father. So it seems obvious to me we should always ask Him to clean up our petitions and remove any traces of dishonour or self-centred, unholy desire, as well as request that He empower our declarations of forgiveness or repentance.

There's an incredibly good reason the Lord's Prayer starts with: *'Hallowed be Your Name.'* If we dishonour God's holiness in prayer, we are targets for retaliation by the Resheph aspect of Leviathan. So many word-of-faith declarations by believers today amount to little more than magical incantations spoken with the intent of wish-fulfilment, not with the intent of God's-will-fulfilment.

There's never a problem with asking for empowerment of repentance or forgiveness, as Ian quickly found. However there is almost invariably a problem otherwise. Our hearts genuinely are deceitful, so asking Jesus to modify, re-word, even delete any unholy parts of the appeal we want Him to present to the Father is always wise.

The Fruit called *self-control* is actually *Spirit-endowed empowerment*. It begins to mature in our lives when we recognise the limits of our own willpower, then turn to Jesus and ask Him to supply what we lack.

When I was working on my theory it would only take six days of sitting in rejection to overcome it, and I was up to eighteen but nothing was happening, God said to me: 'You keep dropping out of the place of rejection. You're defaulting back into handling mode.' That was the moment I realised the brain-pathways of 'handling mode' were so automatic I could never overcome them myself. I needed God's empowerment to stop 'handling'. It's simply a matter of asking for the automatics to be switched off and for Him to take control. Sure, there are times when, unthinking, I've found myself in the old default zone once more—so I ask for forgiveness, I repent and I ask Jesus of Nazareth to empower my words. I speak aloud because, if I don't, I find my thoughts trailing off into a fog and I never finish speaking out the statement I intended.

A war also needs armour for its combatants.

The Armour of God is the divine covering Jesus provides for us through His kiss.[63]

> *The hour has come for you to wake from sleep. For salvation is nearer to us now than when we first believed. The night is far gone; the day is at hand.*

So then let us cast off the works of darkness and put on the armour of light.

Romans 13:11–12 ESV

Just as the Fruit of the Spirit replaces the weaponised fruit from the Tree of the Knowledge of Good and Evil, so this shielding reinstates the skins that humanity wore in Eden. Both the armour and the skins are composed of light. The armour is explicitly stated to be that way. The Hebrew, of course, is less direct in making the connection but Paul has given us a clue in his epistle by linking *waking* to *light*. As it happens, the Hebrew word for the *skins*, 'owr', God gave to Adam and Eve is the same as the word for *wake*, 'ur', and sounds like *light*, 'owr'. (It may seem like in English transliteration that *skin*, 'owr', is identical to *light*, 'owr', and totally different from *wake*, 'ur', but it's the exact opposite, due unfortunately to some very inconsistent practices in the English spelling of Hebrew names and words.)

Beautifully, since the word for *putting on armour* in Hebrew is the same as that for *giving and receiving a kiss*, then Paul's instruction to garb ourselves in the armour of light also means *receive the kiss of Light*.

Our armour-bearer and paraclete gird us with items that are not only a warrior's protective garb but also priestly garments in addition to royal robes. The armour is encrusted with jewels of significance and fragrant with a potent mix of perfumes, as well as splendidly arrayed with musical and mathematical aspects. Most importantly, it is especially designed for crossing thresholds. This is made evident by many double-meanings: *shield*, for example, is also *door* and *arrows* is also *threshold*.

> *Take up the shield of faith, with which you can extinguish all the flaming arrows of the evil one.*

Ephesians 6:16 BSB

In this verse, 'belos' is the Greek word for both *threshold* as well as *arrows* and it is derived from 'ballo', meaning *to throw* or *to cast*. It is related to 'ekballo', *to throw out* or *cast out*. 'Ballo' is what demons consistently do to us. 'Ekballo' is what Jesus consistently did to demons—and, surprisingly, once what the Holy Spirit did to Jesus: straight after His baptism, the Holy Spirit *ekballo*'ed Him into the wilderness.

We need the Armour of God so that whatever is *ballo*'ed at us bounces off and is *ekballo*'ed away without harm. Some believers think that we put on the Armour of God once and it's there for the rest of our lives. Others intentionally put it on, piece by piece, as they start each day. I like to ask for God's kiss for myself, my family and my friends—because Paul's instruction to put on the armour indicates it is collective protection, not just for individuals.

Because this armour is designed especially for crossing thresholds, where the spirit of rejection holds most sway, we need to be careful not to lose it. Or cast it aside through reliance on our own strength.

One day Samson went to the Philistine town of Gaza and spent the night with a prostitute. Word soon spread that Samson was there, so the men of Gaza gathered together and waited all night at the town gates. They kept quiet during the night, saying to themselves, 'When the light of morning comes, we will kill him.'

But Samson stayed in bed only until midnight. Then he got up, took hold of the doors of the town gate, including the two posts, and lifted them up, bar and all. He put them on his shoulders and carried them all the way to the top of the hill across from Hebron.

Judges 16:1–3 NLT

This is the turning point in the story of Samson. Full of dense symbolism, it records the incident that was the direct cause of his downfall. We tend to think it was his relationship with Delilah that was his undoing, but no—just prior to it came this mysterious interlude in Gaza which is the real beginning of the end.

Now, the English name for the town Gaza gives the impression it starts with G. It doesn't. In Hebrew it is simply 'Azzah', from 'az', *strong*.[64] That's right, it's related to Azazel.

Samson the strongman pitted himself against Gaza, *the strong city.* He'd already killed a thousand Philistine princes with the jawbone of a donkey so he had to know he was heading into trouble by entering the stronghold at Gaza. However, he was a judge of Israel—and famous—so finding a prostitute in his own land would have invited scandal and censure.

Perhaps this story of shame would have remained hidden but for the way Samson very cleverly outmanoeuvred the group of assassins waiting at the gate. While he was inside the city, he was protected by a threshold covenant—the pledges of hospitality that ensured peace and mutual defence within the walls. But once he left the city, the covenant would no longer apply: this is why the killers set up their ambush just outside the gates. Apparently the Philistines had integrity—and Samson, aware of this, used it against them. He lifted the gates onto his shoulders, pillars and all, and began carrying them towards Hebron, dozens of kilometres away.

In effect, he was extending the boundaries of the city and, by keeping himself inside, he maintained the covering of the threshold covenant. As soon as he was within sight of Hebron, the guards from this city of refuge would have swarmed to his aid. And while a night with a prostitute was nothing to boast about, taking the gates of an enemy city was such a spectacular achievement it allowed this unsavoury aspect to slip into the background.

Except for one thing.

God is a covenant-keeping God. Manipulating and twisting covenantal obligations to our own advantage is a sure-fire way of pushing Him aside and coming out from under His protection. Remember that immutable law woven into the fabric of the universe? *We reap what we sow.* Samson had activated it in a major way and he no longer had God's strength to defend him, just his own.

Like a geas—the taboo described in Celtic mythology that, if violated, will lead to death—Samson had certain restrictions on his life. As a dedicated Nazarite, his hair could not be cut. He broke many of the vows, but this one he kept—clearly understanding that his seven braids were the secret of augmenting his own strength with divine force.[65]

Right at the end of Samson's story when he was a blind prisoner in Gaza, we are given a clue as to the reap-what-you-sow nature of his life. He had abused threshold covenant and taken the protection of the city. The Philistines had therefore taken his protection, his hair. That *hair*, as it re-grows, is spelled in Hebrew exactly the same way as *gates*.[66] It's an unusual, but perfect, parallel. Significantly both these words, *gates* and *hair*, are related to *goats* and *barley*.

A web of connections then links these back to Azazel. Although *hair* is 'sear' and *gate* is 'shaar' in the English transliterations, ancient Hebrew uses identical spellings for them. Hair is derived from 'sa'ar', *bristle with fear*—evoking images of Pan and Azazel. In turn 'sa'ar' is a variant of 'saar', *storm* or *horror*. The network of meanings extends further: *storm* can also be spelled 'searah', exactly the same in Hebrew as the hairy grain, 'seorah', *barley*.

With all these interwoven aspects, it should come as no surprise that Gaza was once a major barley-exporter.[67] It may be surprising that barley was once seen as a symbol of *strength*, but in the days of the Roman Empire, this was quite normal. Gladiators were known as 'hordearii', *barley men*. The most popular of these celebrity warriors were famous for maintaining their peak physical condition through a diet mainly consisting of barley, wheat and beans.

Azazel's stomping ground at Caesarea Philippi thus naturally became the scene of gladiatorial combat.[68] After the destruction of Jerusalem, some 97,000 captives were caught and sold as slaves or forced to take part in triumphal games to celebrate the Roman victory over the Jews.[69]

There are such obvious spiritual errors in relying in our own strength and willpower, they hardly need to be mentioned. Still, it's worth noting that our dependence on self is utterly entangled with rejection of God. Sometimes this rejection is so deep-seated it's invisible to us. We're unaware of it. This is especially true when we build a false refuge of the good gifts God gives us, rather than flee to Him as our one and only true refuge.

One of the words for *seeking refuge* is in fact 'uz' and, from it comes 'maoz', *stronghold, fortress* or *tower*. At the basis of 'uz' is *to be strong* or to *strengthen* by *gathering the self* and *saving the self by fleeing*.

Azazel, *strength of God*, like the angel called Terror who is tasked with sweeping our enemies before us, was almost certainly once assigned to strengthen mankind and provide refuges for them in war. Instead he schooled humanity in the arts of conflict, gave them the science of metallurgy and weaponry, and terrorised them into fleeing and establishing strongholds that were false refuges.

Today, most of our world is much less frightening than in days gone by. We've tamed so much of it that our false refuges are rarely physical hide-outs: they are instead mental habits, the 'noema' or *strongholds of thought*, that Paul exhorts us to take captive:

> *The weapons of our warfare are not of the flesh but have divine power to destroy strongholds. We destroy arguments and every lofty opinion raised against the knowledge of God, and take every thought captive to obey Christ.*

> 2 Corinthians 10:4–5 ESV

How do we overcome the most stubbornly defiant and securely reinforced of these refuges? By going to the Lord. Sometimes He'll take down our strongholds in one mighty smash—but more often He demolishes them one block at a time.

Prayer

Father in Heaven, I call on Jesus of Nazareth as my mediator and advocate to empower these words and present them to You. Please make them honouring, Jesus. Please ensure they glorify Your Father and mine. Make them clean and undefiled and worthy to be received by heaven and recorded by angels.

Father God, forgive me for failing to rely on You. I so often say I love You. I so often say I trust You. But at the first sign of trouble my prayers become missiles of concentrated worry. You've given me armour; you've given me weapons—but I've failed to understand I need to play my part in maturing the Fruit of love, joy, peace, patience, kindness, goodness, faithfulness, gentleness and self-control. I thought that I could just use my authority as a believer, bind up the spirit of rejection and cast it out. I didn't realise that's an attempt to control, but it's not self-control. I didn't realise I was attempting to exercise power, but not exercise empowerment.

None of my actions demonstrate trust in You or genuine love for You. But You teach me love. You are my paraclete, the one who stands back-to-back with me in the fiercest conflict. You are always my defender—at least You are when I stay within Your covering. You are ready to send

Your Terror before me to drive out my enemies, just so long as I do as I'm told. But I don't. I keep sending up my missiles of concentrated worry to You in prayer. I keep them in a small bag so they are always on hand in times of trouble. They are one of my handiest false refuges.

Father, I repent once more of dishonouring You through the creation of false refuges. I ask Jesus to empower my words and I ask You to forgive me.

Thank You for Your forgiveness and Your cleansing of my spirit, heart and mind. Please refresh me with the Spirit of Jesus so that I have an attitude of gratitude. Allow me to know and show Your peace, love, grace and truth in my life.

Thank You for renewing my mind and transforming me into an image-bearer of Yourself through the power of the cross of Jesus.

In His Name. Amen.

5

The Art of Law

The number one fear in life is rejection. The number one need is acceptance.

Dr Phil McGraw

The deepest principle in human nature is the craving to be appreciated.

William James

Your need for acceptance can make you invisible in this world. Don't let anything stand in the way of the light that shines through this form. Risk being seen in all of your glory.

Jim Carrey

WHEN I BEGAN TO WRITE this book, I started to collect nifty quotes like the ones above. After all, what's a book on rejection without some memorable citations from various celebrities and experts? However, there came the moment when I began to wonder if they were actually right.

As I thought about Moses and Elijah, I realised they were repeatedly offered the unfathomable *acceptance* of covenant but they actually preferred *safety*. And when I mused about that on social media, a very interesting comment came from a woman who'd known my father. When she'd become engaged, she'd told my dad that Tim, her husband-to-be, was in the military. 'Ah,' he said, 'Tim needs to make himself safe, or the world safe.'

Now actually, Moses and Elijah—and for that matter, Cain and Abraham—preferred their own definitions of safety to God's covenantal defence. So 'perceived safety' is probably a better way of describing it. Moses seems to have suffered from abandonment issues and separation anxiety for his entire life. Abraham created his own 'perceived safety' when he went to Gerar and asked Sarah to say she was his sister, not his wife. He'd practised this deception previously in Egypt with serious consequences: plague had fallen on the household of Pharaoh. And when Pharaoh realised and sent Abraham away, his opening words form the first echo in Scripture of God's confrontation of Adam in the Garden of Eden. The second echo occurs when Abraham is confronted by Abimelech, the king of Gerar. God had given Abraham an almost identical test—but Abraham had again chosen to trust his own devices and scheming rather than in God as his promised Shield and Reward.

Although both Pharaoh and Abimelech sent Abraham away with a mountain of gifts, there is no question he was *cast out, exiled, ekballo*'ed. Both monarchs, in their initial shock, poignantly repeat God's words leading up to the expulsion from Eden. The tragedy of Abraham's action is that, in Egypt, he didn't even have a blood covenant with God—but by the time of the incident in Gerar, about twenty-five years later, he had four covenants with God: blood, name, threshold, salt.

As a consequence of his failure to honour these covenants, the test passed down to his son Isaac who found himself in an identical situation—but who did no better. The pattern was so strong by this stage that deception about women became the unresolved issue in the patriarchal family line. Isaac and Rebekah thus named one of their sons for it—Jacob, *deceiver*.

In one generation, the issue was safety—as well as rejection of God's protection in favour of a self-devised scheme. By the third generation, this issue still remained but deception was now twisted into the mix as well.

Cain, too, was a seeker of safety. After he killed Abel, God pronounced judgment on him. It was basically: *reap what you've sown*. Cain had been a farmer; his brother a herdsman. Agriculture requires a fairly settled lifestyle whereas tending flocks entails wandering in search of pasture. The spiritual principle of reaping what we've sown operates in one of two ways:

either

- we become like those we've hated and condemned

or, alternatively,

- we repeatedly draw into our lives the type of people who will treat us in just the same way as we've treated those we've hated and condemned.

For Cain, it was the first. He became a wanderer, just as his brother had been. But, even though he said that his punishment was too great for him to bear, was he concerned about rejection or safety?

> *Behold, this day You have driven me from the face of the earth, and from Your face I will be hidden; I will be a fugitive and a wanderer on the earth, and whoever finds me will kill me.*

Genesis 4:14 BSB

God's gift of a mark to protect Cain from vengeful retribution suggests that safety was his chief and foremost worry. In building the first city,[70] we see his desire to settle again, to cease from wandering, to curtail God's sentence of exile and to create for himself a secure stronghold—a place with walls and gates that can become the very essence of safety along with acceptance and rejection. Those inside, accepted; those outside, rejected.

The rejection experienced by Cain occurs time and again in biblical history. It happens in the story of Hagar and Ishmael.[71] It happens in the story of Jacob and Esau,[72] of Jacob and Leah, of Joseph and his brothers. It happens in the story of Moses and his wife Zipporah, of Moses and his sister Miriam, of Moses and his brother Aaron, of Moses and his cousin Korah, of Moses and his grandson Jonathan. Single-handedly Jonathan destroyed all that his grandfather had worked four decades to achieve—to weld a disparate, raggle-taggle band of slaves into a single brotherhood, a unified nation under God. Not surprisingly, the precipitating incident that led to Jonathan's involvement in bringing about the disintegration of the tribal confederation involved a threshold. Moses could never overcome his fear of thresholds—so the issue passed down his generational line—and eventually created a mess in that 'fine hill country and Lebanon' Moses was so keen to use as a detour into the Promised Land.

Moses reminds me of a woman I knew who asked me to pray for her. She thought that my prayers were unusually powerful and that God would answer my requests swiftly and affirmatively. In her view, He always ignored her. He crushed her enthusiasm and rejected her on multiple levels.

'I will pray in agreement with you,' I told her, 'but not on your behalf. I am not your mediator. Jesus is. If anyone's prayers are powerful, it is His and only His. I'm willing to help you hold the hem of His garment, but I'm not doing it for you.' Some people think I fob them off when I tell them to ask Jesus themselves, but I'm not willing to be put into a position that rightfully belongs only to Him.

In this particular instance, I knew that God really wanted to speak into the core wound of rejection in her life. That was the real issue. Although she was praying for a job, a house and early access to an inheritance, I sensed that what God wanted to say was: *I love you.* So perhaps I should not have been surprised when miracle after miracle occurred and the job, the house and the inheritance all came to pass. God was lavishly, abundantly proclaiming: *I love you, I love you, I love you.*

Yet, about a year after this, it was as if nothing had happened. 'God never answers my prayers,' she said.

Huh? I thought. *How can you have forgotten? The evidence is all around you.*

The inability of Moses to accept God's invitation to cross the threshold reminds me of that. The evidence was all around him. Every day God sent a reminder from heaven in the form of manna about the name covenant He wanted Moses to receive. Manna means *'What is it?'* just as 'mazeh' does. *Cross over,* God was saying, *from an Egyptian name to a Hebrew one. Don't leave your heart in the Black Land.*[73]

Jonathan's story continues the tragedy of Moses and compounds it. Jonathan was the Levite who travelled from Bethlehem to the hill country of Ephraim, stopping at Gibeah overnight. When the men of Gibeah surrounded his lodging and demanded to have sex with him, he threw out his concubine who was gang-raped all night and died at morning light. Her last action was to touch the sacred threshold stone and thereby proclaim that the men in the house sacrificed her, ignoring that they were duty-bound by covenant to protect her.

In the subsequent war instigated by Jonathan,[74] the clans of Benjamin were virtually wiped out and the brotherhood of the twelve tribes was irretrievably broken. In the aftermath of that disaster, Jonathan went north with an invasion force from Dan. His descendants set up an idolatrous sanctuary, complete with golden calves, just a short distance from Caesarea Philippi.

The defilement in this area was so great that, century after century, it drew those individuals and families dominated by the spirit of rejection into its sphere of influence, constantly reinforcing the corruption and deepening it. Yet, never forget, this is the place where Jesus spoke His church into being; this is the place He declared war on the principalities of the nations; this is the place He began His campaign against the young lions.

This is also the place where He welcomed Simon as the first member of His church with the name Cephas, *cornerstone*. And the place where His mission to Calvary was rejected:

> *Kefa took Him aside and began rebuking Him, 'Heaven be merciful, Lord! By no means will this happen to You!'*
>
> *But Yeshua turned His back on Kefa, saying, 'Get behind Me, Satan! You are an obstacle in My path,*

because your thinking is from a human perspective, not from God's perspective!'

Matthew 16:22–23 CJB

Correction is not rejection. Still, what the events of Caesarea Philippi tell us, over and over again, is that the way to acceptance passes over rejection.

If you pour out affirmation on an unbroken root of rejection, it only feeds the arrogance, pride and ambition that have been constructed to cover that root.

R. Loren Sandford,
Calling, Wilderness and Return:
Purifying the Prophetic[75]

Tiny babies do not have the cognitive skills to understand adoption. What they sense is imprinted on their hearts from their earliest days: my mother has abandoned me, my parents have rejected me, my family have discarded me, something is wrong with me.

Adopted children frequently have a core wounding— an injury to their very inmost being. Their hearts are broken and they don't think they can be fixed. So they develop coping mechanisms to deal with the rejection.

It's not only adopted children who grow up with a deep sense of rejection. Sometimes, when a baby is adopted and brought into an existing family, the other children can feel obscurely threatened. This is particularly true if the other children are very young and not adopted. A two-year-old suddenly having to share space with an adopted baby may wonder: 'What's wrong with me? There must be something, otherwise my parents wouldn't have looked for a better child. Why have they rejected me?' Such two-year-olds are rarely able to articulate such feelings, even for decades, and are often baffled by the sense of wrongness and rejection that continually overwhelms them.

Long before that, however, they've developed similar coping skills to their adopted siblings. We've noted some of these before:

- Flight. We can flee from the problem—but it's always going to follow us. That's the way Pan operates. We think we can escape Azazel by ducking into a refuge, but that's what he wants.

- Fight. 'What we resist persists.' We can try fighting this spirit but we won't get far. Beating Azazel into submission in our own strength isn't likely to succeed. And if it does, he will soon be back with a band of allies: in particular, the spirit of abuse, the spirit of wasting, the vampire spirit.

- Freeze. We can just stop and hope our statue-like stillness is going to save us. But all this does is play into the hands of Azazel's ally, the spirit of wasting.

- Forget. We can try to ignore it. We can hope it will go away if we sideline it and don't think about it. But, behind our backs, it's just growing monstrously big.

- Forestall. We can pre-empt rejection by anticipating it and getting in first. This enables us to pretend we weren't rejected; but it doesn't really heal the core wounding of our hearts.

- Flatter. We can try to prevent rejection by fawning over those we want to accept us. But friendships grow strong and vigorous through honesty, not flattery.

We need to remember that, what we fear, we create. Instead of these inadequate methods of dealing with rejection, we need to:

- Face it squarely.

Sit down with Jesus, so He can help us work through the fear and the panic, the emotional turmoil and the frenzied sense of being hunted. Sometimes this may involve fasting, since it is in reference to the spirit that Jesus rebuked at Caesarea Philippi that He said, *'This kind does not come out except by prayer and fasting.'*

Note that Jesus didn't bind this spirit, nor did He cast it out. He rebuked it.

It should be noted that the Greek word for *rebuke*, 'epitimao', is derived from *honour*. His actions are thus fully in accord with the recommendations about not dishonouring angelic majesties in Jude 1:9–11 and 2 Peter 2:11–12; indicating there is a difference in spiritual strategy we should employ between fallen powers and their demonic offspring.[76]

For many years, I had a nightmare where I was relentlessly chased by a monstrous tree. Somehow, over time, I came to know the name of the tree. And when I encountered the image of the pursuer 'Bran' in the poetry of Clive Hamilton, a pen-name of CS Lewis, I immediately recognised the name and what his hunter symbolised. Now Lewis told me something in his poetry that I had never realised in the dream: the dream-hunter never catches up with you because its agenda is far more subtle and sinister: *it follows after in order to undo the good that you do.*

Although Scripture doesn't reveal this about Azazel, nor does the information appear in any of the legends of Pan, I nonetheless believe that Lewis' insight was perfectly correct: the spirit of rejection follows after you to undo the good that you do throughout your life. That's its purpose—to pull down any spiritual legacy you might create that would cause blessings to flow to the next generation.

Whatever name your personal spirit happens to know the soul-hunter by—Azazel, Samyaza, Pan, Capricorn,[77] Bran[78] or any other cultural variant[79]—it wants to chase you into a false refuge and, while you're there, it will be unravelling all you've achieved for the Kingdom of God. It will take the opportunity while you're nestling down into your foxhole and communing with your idols of comfort and consolation, to tear down your attainments.

One of the greatest tragedies in Scripture was the demolition of all Moses achieved in his lifetime by his grandson Jonathan. In Judges 18:30, Jonathan is identified as the apostate Levite who sacrificed his concubine to save himself, who stole silver idols and an ephod, and whose descendents set up a golden calf at a sanctuary in Dan, not far from Caesarea Philippi. When we reject the threshold covenant of God, we reject the divine protection and defence that comes with it. In doing so, we lay ourselves open to having the good that we've done for the kingdom of God undone by the spirit of rejection. This unravelling may happen for us in our own lifetime or, as it transpired for Moses, beyond it: the trauma that prevented Moses from accepting God's offer of a new name and a pair of covenants still profoundly affected the third generation, with consequences that ripped the nation apart.

'A good person leaves an inheritance for their children's children.'

Proverbs 13:22 NIV

This includes a spiritual inheritance, full of blessing. Often it's difficult to see that our achievements are collapsing behind us because, remember, soul-hunters are also spell-binders. It's difficult to be sure what the concept of 'spell-binding' originally meant but a reasonable guess is that it was about the power of words to control the minds of others. This is not about a cogent argument to influence opinion, this is about manipulation of truth.

Spell-binding, at its simplest level, may be as thoughtless as extracting a promise not to talk about a particular matter. When such promises cause internal conflicts regarding personal integrity—forcing people to choose between keeping their word and speaking out a truth—it's crossed a dangerous line. People who guard such secrets then have to discern whether the greater harm will come from speaking truth or concealing it.

Spell-binding, at its second level, can be a means of coercive control. 'Cancel culture' maximises such techniques. But it's far from the only place it operates. Sometimes a leader may extract a promise of silence as an instinctive way of controlling criticism or manipulating a particular outcome. But then a fine line is established between rejecting alternate views and rejecting the other person. When we don't value people enough to listen to them and welcome their input, then we dishonour them. And our prayers may well be hindered.

Spell-binding, at a still higher level, can move to spiritual tyranny. God always gives us the privilege of saying 'no'; He always gives us a choice. So any document or statement that has been deliberately crafted to give the receiver no right of reply or appeal, no recourse to justice or mediation, no choices or options except the outcome the sender wants, falls into this category. In rejecting and devaluing the rights of others, the spell-crafter has moved beyond fleshly control and psychological or emotional mistreatment to spiritual tyranny and abuse.[80]

Spell-binding that goes one step further to involve mind control is pure, unadulterated malice. Sometimes this will involve drugs. After all, *drugs* are what 'root-cutting' implies, and 'root-cutting' is the other art, besides spell-binding, that the angelic rebel Samyaza taught to humanity.

Maybe *drugs* and *spell-binding* don't seem such a likely combination today. Yet there was an ancient word that brought the two ideas together in a single word: 'pharmakeia', *sorcery*.

I was in the Scottish Borders with a free half-day. *Where would I go?* I just couldn't decide. A name I'd seen on a sign flickered into my thoughts. I discarded it. But it came right back. So, on a strange impulse, I did a u-turn and headed for Soutra Aisle.

These stone ruins happen to be the only visible remains of an 'aisle' built by the Pringle family—they are not a church, though they're often described as such. Rather an 'aisle' is a place for consecrated burial. There was a long history of religious construction on this site dating back to a twelfth century Augustinian monastery. I poked around for a bit and was just leaving when a half dozen cars arrived. So I went back to see what was going on.

It turned out that an annual lecture was about to be delivered on this windswept ridge. The topic was fascinating: it was about the herb garden of the medieval monastery—and the plants that still survived in the vicinity, including some from the Himalayas! This had been a very famous monastery—with people coming from all over Europe for cures—and, even in the twenty-first century, there was more than academic interest in these old herbal recipes treasured by the monks. Pharmaceutical companies were investing in research into monastery gardens like Soutra Aisle—because, let's face it, people don't travel from the far ends of Europe to a freezing monastery on a bare ridge in the Scots Lowlands unless there was a genuine hope the monks could produce a cure. And people certainly did recover because the monastery became wealthy through their gifts of gratitude.

The monks of the medieval world believed that God created had not only created everything good, but He had created herbs and plants, roots and leaves that could heal every disease. I think they were right.

When I was growing up, a vaccine was a preventative—both against getting a disease and against spreading the disease. Sometime in the last few decades, the meaning of 'vaccine' changed so that it's simply a jab that ameliorates the symptoms—not an inoculation that delivers old-style immunity.[81] It has in fact become what used to be called a 'treatment', however many people in my age group still understand it with its former meaning. In the Year of Fear 2020, the obsession with a 'vaccine' solution reached almost idolatrous levels as possible non-vaccine treatments were actively destroyed.

Now I'm not a doctor, but I do know this: it wouldn't make any difference if I was. An ordinary general practitioner has no more expertise than I do. Any attempt to navigate the truth about the present array of coronavirus vaccines—or any other for that matter—is impossible. There are scientists with impeccable credentials who are both for and against vaccines; there are eminent researchers on both sides of the debate.

Back when I taught science, I always started my first class for the year with the following announcement: 'Two-thirds of what I am about to teach you this year is absolute and total trash.' That would always cause a fair bit of murmuring before I went on: 'Unfortunately, no one will know which two-thirds is wrong until a century after we're all dead.'

The moment I hear the words, *'The science is settled,'* I shake my head in amazement. As we look back on the textbooks of the early twentieth century, it's evident how far knowledge has advanced. Or try looking back on the predictions of the last few decades and see the divergence between reality and projection.

Science isn't settled; it progresses through creating and testing a hypothesis, and then through the independent verification and reproduction of results. The best science engages meticulous counter-testing and continued questioning and refining.

Whenever a theory or a practice is regarded as beyond questioning or valid debate, it is no longer science but religious ideology. Certain 'vaccine' regimes fall into this category: they are now more faith-based than rigorously and independently tested.

They cannot be questioned and, if they are, vitriol is forthcoming. This is a controversial topic but I have grown suspicious when abusive name-calling substitutes for an answer. That strikes me as an attempt at control. Anyone who cannot provide transparent responses in reasoned discourse is, in my view, not to be totally trusted: it's unclear whether they are marketing propaganda, or promoting facts.

We've had years of peddling different sorts of fear—to the point where now much of society gives their vote to the person who makes them feel most 'safe'. When we look at our world today we see the activity of Azazel on a global level, no longer just an individual one. Enormous fear and panic has been created about a pandemic that is hardly 'pan-', that is *all-encompassing*, not when—at the time of writing—2.1% of the 1.1% of the world who have contracted it have died.[82] Death is always a fearful prospect; yes. But this is manufactured, artificially inflated fear.

Our workplaces and governments are moving beyond mind control to physical control as they seek to mandate an experimental pharmaceutical injection. In so many places, the health of a community has narrowed down to a single measure: COVID or not-COVID.

Truly, use your God-given discernment: if the Holy Spirit says to get a vaccine, get it. If He doesn't, don't. Don't forget *syringe* is named for 'syrinx', the instrument of Pan. Make God your governor, no one else.

Let's talk covenant.

Today's world aims to maximise division. *'We're all in this together,'* proclaim the ads on television. But one thing is for sure: we're not all in this together. At no time in the history of the world have responsible governments said to be more afraid.

'We have nothing to fear but fear itself,' said Franklin Delano Roosevelt in his inaugural presidential address but the sentiment had been around for nearly five centuries.

Responsible government does not feed fear. It tells us to take care, to be courageous in the face of danger, to take no unnecessary risks, to consider all aspects of healthcare and not just one. It guards and watches over the economic welfare of all its citizens and it is vigilant in terms of overseeing business and does not assume that multi-national global enterprises will act ethically, in the best interests of all, and will never try to get away with whatever short-cuts they can, in pursuit of a higher profit margin. It is naïve to think otherwise.

Marketing experts tell us that, to sell product, it's necessary to create a need. Fear, of course, instantly creates a high-level need: *freedom* from fear. When we're abjectly worrying, panicking wildly, freezing in fright, fleeing in terror, hurriedly devising some fool-proof plan to flatter, fawn, forestall or forget the problem, we're falling in with the agenda of the spirit of rejection. Ultimately, we're covenanting with it, rather than with Jesus.

The essential nature of covenant is oneness. Covenant is often mistaken for a particularly solemn set of vows and obligations. But the crucial difference between contract and covenant lies in its 'diversified unity': that is, in a oneness that is not conformity, but a bringing-together, as in parts of the Body.

The threshold covenant originated in hospitality and had a specialised sense of oneness. It was about defence, essentially saying to a guest: *anyone who attacks you attacks me. I will defend you in the same way as I would defend myself. I will expend all I have to protect you, sacrificing my family for your safety. I expect the same from you.*

To partake in this covenant, a guest simply had to pass over the cornerstone, step into the house and receive the kiss of greeting from the host and perhaps some anointing oil for the head and water for the feet. In the unlikely event a guest wanted to refuse covenant, he would kick the cornerstone, or strike it, or dash his foot against it or hit it: all these Scriptural descriptions are not so much about stumbling by accident but about refusing covenant. It was about saying: *no, I don't want any obligation of mutual defence.*

When Jesus set up His church in the most hostile territory on the planet, He created a threshold by giving Simon the name Cephas, *cornerstone*, then He went up the Mount of Assembly to demonstrate that His defence of His people would be all-embracing. Not one principality would speak against the Father's chosen Son. Elijah and Moses might converse with Him but their very appearance testifies to a security they never felt in their own time on earth.

All of this takes place in territory dominated by various shrines and temples devoted to imagery of Azazel throughout many centuries and across different cultures. It's not just about the cornerstone and the threshold covenant that is intrinsic to the passover of the cornerstone, it's also about rejection.

> *This Jesus is 'the stone you builders rejected, which has become the cornerstone.'*

Acts 4:11 BSB

This is the mind-warping paradox. Covenant is oneness; but the spirit of rejection wants us to believe that rejection is the opposite of oneness. That it's always always always about separation and division. Normally, of course, it is. But with God, acceptance and rejection come into logic-defying unity when we accept the name and threshold covenant Jesus offers us. Then we are invited to come into oneness with the One who was rejected and yet became the Chief Cornerstone. The deeper our intimacy with Jesus the more we will experience the paradox of rejection that defies separation.

This paradox is why, I believe, Jesus rebuked the spirit of Pan but didn't cast it out. This is why, I believe, that God told Cain to subdue the sin that crouched at his door. This is why, I believe, so many people who try to bind the spirit of rejection simply find it lies low for a few months before disrupting their lives once more.

The closer we get to Jesus with our coping mechanisms still intact, the more we'll find panic rises and we act out rejection towards others. Allow Him to dismantle the coping mechanisms and simply sit with Him until He completes the work.

One crucial point regarding this completed work: I may be wrong but I do not think we can ever say that rejection has been forever removed from our lives. That would be to suggest we do not share in an integral aspect of who Jesus is. I believe God said to overcome this spirit because we are not so much called to cast it out as master it.

A second crucial point: we can mistake the *memory* of rejection for the *spirit* of rejection. Be discerning. All too often we react to a memory activated by the spirit, rather than the spirit itself. Think of someone who has had a leg amputated but is crippled by debilitating phantom pains. The problem is obviously not the leg, since it's no longer there. The issue is the stored memory of the trauma. The brain is a filing system: it records, not the memory itself, but where in the body the memory is stored. This may sound like a big problem but it's not: we can simply pray for the memory of the trauma to be lifted out of the organ where it's located.

This is a vitally important consideration regarding rejection: the core wounding needs to be addressed because even when the spirit is mastered, the traumatic memory still exists. Thus sometimes the spirit will try to re-establish ascendancy in our lives because the memory has not received prayer.

But what if we can't remember? For some people, whole years of their lives are a total blank. We can still ask the Holy Spirit to go to the site of the memory and heal it. Sometimes it may be necessary to remember, so ask Him to restore the memory without pain. Sometimes it may not. Be guided by the One who knows how to heal every disease and every affliction of mind and heart.

Prayer

Father and Protector, may Your name be ever honoured and glorified. May Jesus be my mediator in prayer and may He filter my words so that they always lift up Your name.

Lord, I acknowledge that so much of my life has been spent reacting to fear—

: the fear of being rejected.

: the fear of being shamed.

: the fear of being wrong.

: the fear of not having enough.

: the fear of serious illness.

: the fear of being seen.

: the fear of not being seen.

: the fear of losing my job.

The list is endless. Fear, it's said, is faith in evil that hasn't happened yet. It is entertaining a fantasy about a danger that may never occur. Abba, fear truly is faith in the power of the evil one—the opposite from faith in You. Time and time again I have indulged in the helplessness of fear to avoid taking action. I am sorry and I ask Your pardon.

Abba, the worry and anxiety resulting from fear has so often incapacitated me and kept me from turning to You in wholehearted faith, trust and love. I've chosen to utilise one of my coping mechanisms instead of looking to You—the One who is Love and who casts out all fear.

Your Word says that we *reap what we sow* and, Abba Father, I acknowledge the truth of that statement: by sowing fear I have reaped an abundance of things to be ever more fearful about. Your Word is Truth and we who worship You must worship in Spirit and in Truth.

Abba, I repent and I ask Jesus to empower my repentance. I also ask Your Holy Spirit to block my way at the first sign of turning to the false refuge of fear. It does nothing except destroy my relationship with You and Your Son, Jesus, and I ask that You cleanse the parts of my heart that secretly want to hold on my false refuges so that I can be the one in control of my life.

I thank You for Your forgiveness, Father, in the name of Jesus, Your Son, my Lord and the everlasting Head of the body of Christ. Amen.

6

The Art of Dawn

READING WITH THE TEXT, NOT THE HERO is perhaps the most important principle we can bring to our study of the Bible.[83] Jesus said, *'No one is good except God alone,'*[84] but we tend to put a halo on the designated heroes and question the motives of their opponents, rather than take a serious look at their own.

There's a special word for this human tendency to elevate culture heroes to god-like status: it's called *euhemerism.* It is fine to look up our leaders, honour them and want to emulate them—but that is no longer the case when any admiration of their better qualities twists into hero worship so unbridled that all their character flaws are overlooked. We enshrine or enthrone our idols, allowing them to usurp the rightful place of God in our lives.[85]

In the time of Jesus, Moses had been turned into a culture hero who had dispensed bread from heaven: we know this because Jesus had to state, *'Truly, truly, I tell you, it was not Moses who gave you the bread from heaven, but it is My Father who gives you the true bread from heaven.'*[86] We don't need to ignore the flaws of the heroes of the faith; we need to recognise that they, like us, need healing and that God loves us anyway.

All this by way of preamble to a story about David, Israel's second king.

At some point in his reign David decided to bring the Ark of the Covenant to Jerusalem. Perhaps he consulted God, but there is no mention of it. He did, however, consult the people: tens of thousands of them from Syria to Egypt.

> *David conferred with each of his officers, the commanders of thousands and commanders of hundreds. He then said to the whole assembly of Israel, 'If it seems good to you and if it is the will of the Lord our God, let us send word far and wide to the rest of our people throughout the territories of Israel, and also to the priests and Levites who are with them in their towns and pasturelands, to come and join us. Let us bring the ark of our God back to us, for we did not inquire of it during the reign of Saul.' The whole assembly agreed to do this, because* **it seemed right to all the people***.*

> *So David assembled all Israel, from the Shihor River in Egypt to Lebo Hamath, to bring the ark of God from Kiriath Jearim. David and all Israel went to Baalah of Judah (Kiriath Jearim) to bring up from there the ark of God the Lord, who is enthroned between the cherubim—the ark that is called by the Name.*

They moved the ark of God from Abinadab's house on a new cart, with Uzzah and Ahio guiding it. David and all the Israelites were celebrating with all their might before God, with songs and with harps, lyres, timbrels, cymbals and trumpets.

When they came to the threshing floor of Kidon, Uzzah reached out his hand to steady the ark, because the oxen stumbled. The Lord's anger burned against Uzzah, and he struck him down because he had put his hand on the ark. So he died there before God.

Then David was angry because the Lord's wrath had broken out against Uzzah, and to this day that place is called Perez Uzzah.

David was afraid of God that day and asked, 'How can I ever bring the ark of God to me?'

1 Chronicles 13:1–12 NIV

This is the parallel reading from the book of Chronicles to the passage we looked at earlier from 2 Samuel 6. It adds a bit more detail: it reveals that the entire nation was assembled for this ceremony. It strongly suggests this was a political event, staged more for the enhancement of David's prestige than for the honour of God. It mentions that *all* the people thought David's proposal was right. It tells us that David asked, *'How can I ever bring the ark of God **to me**?'* thereby hinting with those last two words that this was less for the protection of the kingdom than the protection of the king.

David's fear of God was mixed with anger. He wasn't immediately humbled by the holiness of God. I believe his anger was born out of shame. He'd been humiliated before a vast multitude of people when Uzzah died. Despite making a great occasion of the transferral from Kiriath-Jearim to Jerusalem, despite celebrating with all their might, despite their overwhelmingly good intentions—because I do believe that, despite the untoward motives, most of David's intentions were honourable—disaster occurred. Uzzah died.[87] He was, in effect, as his name suggests, David's scapegoat and in some way the scapegoat for the entire nation. The priests and the Levites were called up with the rest of the assembly: they should have told David how God wanted His Ark to be moved from place to place.

But David's scapegoating didn't stop with Uzzah.

Ted Peters in *Sin: Radical Evil in Soul and Society*[88] describes the descent into evil as roughly moving through the following seven stages:

- Anxiety
- Unfaith
- Pride
- Concupiscence
- Scapegoating
- Cruelty
- Blasphemy

First is *anxiety* which prepares us to turn against God. Second is *unfaith*, a term Peters coined himself, to describe a state which is far beyond doubt—it is a catastrophic loss of faith in God's goodness. Third is the self-explanatory *pride*. Fourth is *concupiscence*, a word normally associated with sexual desire but in this case describing insatiable lust for power over people, programmes or projects in any kind of public or private sphere. Fifth is *scapegoating*—in its modern sense of passing the blame to someone else. Sixth, *cruelty:* again fairly self-explanatory. Seventh, *blasphemy:* here symbols are reversed so that good becomes evil and evil becomes good.

Without an understanding of this last step in all its horror, we cannot really grasp the nature of the spiritual counterfeits in the world today. So many believers allow the satan to get away with theft because they agree that certain symbols belong to him, when in fact they are stolen property and rightly belong to God. Jesus came to return all things to their rightful owner and we are called to cooperate with Him in this work of redemption, not side with the enemy.

Now, as Peters pointed out, the seven stages into deepening sin are not necessarily in order all the time for every person. Nonetheless in David's reaction to Uzzah's death, I believe we can see *anxiety, unfaith*—a loss of faith in God's favour, if not goodness or holiness—and *pride*. Subsequent events indicate he progressed further along the stages. The Ark stayed three months with Obed-Edom and, seeing the blessing that resulted in that household, David tried again.

Wearing a linen ephod, David was dancing before the Lord with all his might, while he and all Israel were bringing up the ark of the Lord with shouts and the sound of trumpets.

As the ark of the Lord was entering the City of David, Michal daughter of Saul watched from a window. And when she saw King David leaping and dancing before the Lord, she despised him in her heart.

They brought the ark of the Lord and set it in its place inside the tent that David had pitched for it, and ...when David returned home to bless his household, Michal daughter of Saul came out to meet him and said, 'How the king of Israel has distinguished himself today, going around half-naked in full view of the slave girls of his servants as any vulgar fellow would!'

David said to Michal, 'It was before the Lord, who chose me rather than your father or anyone from his house when he appointed me ruler over the Lord's people Israel—I will celebrate before the Lord. I will become even more undignified than this, and I will be humiliated in my own eyes. But by these slave girls you spoke of, I will be held in honour.'

And Michal daughter of Saul had no children to the day of her death.

2 Samuel 6:14–23 NIV

Finally, someone with the guts to speak truth to power.

David doesn't deny he was half-naked. In fact, he reacts to the unexpected humiliation this time by declaring he doesn't care about shame: he's going to go for it. He'd do it again, and more! After all, it is in front of the Ark of the Covenant—*'before the Lord'.*

Yet this is the same Lord who, in Exodus 20:26, instructed the people to build a ramp, rather than steps, going up to an altar—so that God would not be dishonoured even by an accidental exposure of nakedness.

There's no excuse for Michal despising David. But there's no excuse either for David's reply. Rather than repenting, he doubled down on his defence—and insulted his wife by saying the slave girls liked the view they got. Did God keep Michal from having children after that? Perhaps. Or was it that David was so angry and unforgiving he never approached her again? Perhaps.

Either way, David's attitude was not right. We can tell because of later events. The Ark of the Covenant is, of course, emblematic of God's covenant with the people. Dishonour to the Ark indicated his heart was not genuinely attuned to honouring covenant. And so, eventually, during a crisis, David broke his covenant with the House of Saul by handing over seven males to be sacrificed by the Gibeonites.

Political expediency meant that he wiped out Michal's wider family, removed any possible threat to his throne and dynasty from Saul's line, and totally dishonoured both God and the nation of Israel by allowing human sacrifice during the barley harvest. Yet again, David— the king who in his beautiful psalms seems to be so deeply in touch with the heart of God—simply didn't *fully* consult with the Lord.

So, more than once in his life, he used others as his scapegoats. Like the rest of us, he heard the start of a word from the Lord but then, on most occasions, he went off and did what was right in his own eyes.

The reason I think we can be sure David dishonoured the House of Saul to an appalling degree is because of the actions of Jesus. In my view, Jesus only healed the history that needed healing. He was usually so subtle about it that, unless we are given the name of the location where He performed His miracles, it's difficult to see the link between His action and past trauma in the landscape.

However, the degree to which Jesus honoured Saul indicates how badly David had messed up, and had defiled the kingship flowing from him, as well as mutilating covenant. Sure David repented, but in a way that created the precedent that a king could break covenant and then simply repent. The details about Jesus honouring Saul are too long and complex to repeat here but, if you are interested in examining them, they are given in the previous book in this series.[89]Basically, the story of Lazarus involves honouring the House of Saul. This would not have needed to happen if David had repaired the breach he had created.

We may actually wonder, at this point, how David could possibly be a *'man after God's own heart'.* I think it was simply because he wanted to keep covenant. He did it badly, he failed, but he repented and tried again. God is a covenant-keeping God and this is what He wants of His people.

This book is about threshold covenant and one of the spirits that makes it so horrendously difficult for us to pass over the threshold into our calling. God wants us to keep threshold covenant because it's disastrous for us and those around us if we don't.

Blood covenant is entirely a work of God—it is 'salvation'—and all of the obligations are on God's side. We cannot add to it, we cannot subtract from it. It is grace through-and-through and beginning-to-end—we can't break it because we didn't have any part in making it. Just as Abram was asleep when God cut a blood covenant with him, so we are asleep, dead in our sins, when God raises a blood covenant with us.

But also just as Abraham was awake for the subsequent covenants—name, threshold, salt—so we are expected to be awake for the subsequent covenants as well.[90] And now the obligations are mutual; now we are a fellow-worker with God in walking out our calling and, if we ignore the promptings of His Spirit, we are stepping out from under His covenantal defence. Curses can rain down on us like missiles and set our lives ablaze.

The spirit of rejection sees our exposed back and shoots for the target. And Azazel sets us up at times. In Jewish mystical texts,[91] Azazel is called the 'seed of Lilith'—and certainly this spirit is one of its allies.[92] In my view its closest ally is Belial, the spirit of abuse,[93] but it is also supported by Ziz, the spirit of forgetting, as well as Leviathan.

In fact, one of the most common set-ups is 'the Leviathan prayer'. I dub it 'the Leviathan prayer' because the snare at the heart of it always involves intense peer pressure to pray in a manner that will dishonour Leviathan. A friend wrote: 'A fellow companion insisted that I pray with her about dealing with Leviathan at the edge of the Sea of Galilee... To my shame, I said a prayer, and... I knew that I was in deep waters... The shame of rejection and lack of self-worth has been rampant in my family bloodline. I think the pressure to conform when the fear of shame and rejection is there is a matter to take to the Lord. Not just the shame of rejection but the way that shame can be manipulated to push you into a trap.'

Another woman who, along with her mother, was pressured into such a prayer found herself asking for help within hours—her mother was taken in a critical condition in an intensive care unit. Yet another woman suffered a fatal fall after leading a group of believers into a temple to curse the demon there. These women all knew better. They knew the warnings, but allowed themselves to be swayed in the pressure of the moment.

To many onlookers the tragedies and near-tragedies that followed may seem 'coincidental'. Yet the very fact we can describe the situations as *tragedies* suggests the influence of Azazel. The word *tragedy* comes from a Greek word for *goat*.[94]

Moreover Scripture repeatedly testifies that, when we know better than to pray in an ignoble way about fallen angelic powers, we invite swift retaliation. Swifter still comes reprisal for dishonouring God in prayer—as shown by the examples of Korah, Dathan and Abiram who were swallowed up in an earthquake, Uzziah who broke out in leprosy, Jeroboam whose hand withered, and Nadab and Abihu who died in a fiery conflagration. In a similar vein of dishonour, there was Belshazzar who defiled the Temple vessels along with Uzzah, of course, who simply tried to stop the Ark from toppling off the cart—as well as Ananias and Sapphira who lied to the Holy Spirit.

Honour is of utmost importance to God. It is also, not surprisingly, important to the threshold guardians— even the fallen ones.

Rejection has enormous generational consequences. Abraham, as we have seen, never resolved his lack of trust in God that led to issues of deception involving women. His failure to pass a second test in this regard led to deception involving women passing down his family line.

But there was also another unresolved issue besides deception. It was rejection, and it too passed down the generations. Abraham was an immensely wealthy man but he sent his son Ishmael away with no more food and water than could be carried on a person's back. Not even a camel or a donkey for provisions, let alone the flocks Abraham helped his nephew Lot acquire. In fact, an honoured overnight visitor was likely to have received more in gifts than Ishmael and his abused mother Hagar did when they were cast out. God may have told Abraham to send Ishmael away as Sarah had said but He didn't say to reject and neglect him. His sons born to Keturah after Sarah's death are also sent away, but not so shamefully. Instead they were piled with gifts.

The issue of the rejected brother thus becomes a feature of Abraham's lineage: first it's Ishmael vs Isaac, then in the next generation Esau vs Jacob, and in the following generation Joseph vs his brothers. Eventually, in the time of the judges and the kings, it becomes a war between the tribe of Judah and the tribe of Benjamin (specifically the people of Bethlehem vs the people of Gibeah, epitomised in the conflict between their respective representatives: David and Saul) and ultimately, of course, the split between the southern kingdom of Judah and that of the northern kingdom, often called Ephraim.

Just as Jacob was called by a name evoking *deceiver*— indicating the unresolved issue of deception in the family line—so Esau has a name evoking *scapegoat* for the unresolved issue of rejection. Esau was also called Seir, *hairy*, which is also a word for *goat*. In fact, Jacob used goatskin gloves to deceive his blind and elderly father in order to get the blessing of the firstborn. Later in life, in a clear example of sowing and reaping, a goat would be used to deceive him when Joseph's coat-of-many-colours was brought to him stained with a goat's blood.[95]

Esau's name comes from 'asah', *to make* or *create*, and that sounds very similar to 'azzah', *goat*. Yet as we've seen, 'azzah' also means *strength*. And that was Esau all over—the one who relied on his own strength to get what he wanted. He was so very much the doer, the hunter—another goat image in its suggestion of Pan. To reinforce the hints of rejection in the name, 'asah' has the same meaning as Cain, *to make, create, fabricate, acquire*. Thus, even though Esau was his father's favourite, his name has faint overtones of the first person to receive God's advice about rejection. And he is pushed aside: his mother and brother conspired to scam him out of the blessing of the firstborn. He so obviously desired acceptance: as soon as he realised his parents objected to his Canaanite wives, he married his cousin Mahalath.[96] Yet rejection was so much part of the family make-up it was no wonder he struggled to accept himself, and consequently despised his birthright, selling it for a bowl of red.

His nephews—the brothers of Joseph—were, like him, rejected by one of their parents. When Simeon was under arrest in Egypt, Jacob accused them:

'You have deprived me of my sons. Joseph is gone and Simeon is no more. Now you want to take Benjamin. Everything is going against me!... My son will not go down there with you, for his brother is dead, and he alone is left. If any harm comes to him on your journey, you will bring my gray hair down to Sheol in sorrow.'

Genesis 42:36–38 BSB

Look at the words: *he alone is left.*

So very similar to Elijah's words: *I alone am left.*

For Jacob, it was as if none of his sons existed, except for Benjamin. His heart was revealed in that moment of grief: only the children of Rachel mattered. None of the others counted. He rejected his wives—Leah, Bilhah and Zilpah—as well as their children. It took a few generations but, inevitably, the descendants of Benjamin became the rejected ones.

And so it goes into our own time: rejection begets rejection. The spirit of rejection inflaming it all further.

So, as I asked in the prologue, *what should we do about the goat?*

Some friends who regularly visit Israel told me about one particular orthodox Jewish sect that practices a ritual with strong echoes of the ancient practice of scapegoating. In the absence of a Temple there is no opportunity for a new high priest to cast lots on Yom

Kippur. It's not possible to choose one goat for sacrifice and one goat to send away into the wilderness with the sins of the people laid on its head. So instead the heads of families in this sect lay the sin of each family on the head of a rooster.[97] Then they kill the rooster and present it as a gift to the poor.

The idea, of course, is that the food will be eaten and the poor person will take in the sin. This effectively—and repugnantly—combines scapegoating with the ancient practice of sin-eating. It is therefore also related to the idea of covenant. And covenant is the reason behind the prohibition of the early church regarding eating meat sacrificed to idols. After all, 'we are what we eat', so if we ingest food that is devoted to a deity and is also designed to make us one with that goddess or godling, then we are effectively agreeing to a covenant.

In a similar way, when we take the sins of others upon ourselves, into our own body, we practice 'sin-eating'.[98] We can also practice 'disease-eating' and take the consequences of other people's actions onto our own spirit. This is not only usurping the role of Jesus as saviour, it is reflective of our lack of trust in the all-sufficiency of His atoning Blood. We don't need to help Jesus save others—either physically or spiritually. He simply doesn't need our assistance. In fact, our assistance is a hindrance.

Sin-eating isn't uncommon. It's easy to participate in it unknowingly through fleshly pity or unredeemed burden-bearing. Azazel can often use such unholy aspects of our nature by promoting a religious agenda.

People often talk about cutting themselves off from those around them whom they perceive have a 'spirit of religion'. Now, there is one particular threshold spirit that we are told we can separate ourselves from, but it isn't this one. The spirit of religion is the spirit of rejection is the spirit of panic is the spirit of marginalisation is the spirit of lust is the spirit of scapegoating. These aren't different spirits: the descriptors simply indicate different aspects to the agenda of Azazel.

Now when believers speak of set free from a 'religious spirit', generally they mean they have been released from a certain way of thinking. This may be as serious as mind control by a dominating church or captivating leader, or it might more likely be that they've at last ditched the idea that obedience to the rules or to a particular tradition will make a salvific difference in their relationship with God.

But these don't necessarily involve a 'religious spirit'. They are simply unbelief in the atonement. It's possible, in fact it's even likely, that Azazel will attach himself to that unbelief and empower it. But that doesn't mean the spirit departs when the belief is discarded. In fact, we can see how deeply Azazel is embedded in people's lives when they start rejecting others they perceive still operate under a religious spirit.[99]

The three markers of a true 'religious spirit' are sacrifice, separation and sorcery. These very aspects are displayed by Azazel:

- sacrifice is what all of the threshold spirits want, since such worship raises a covenant with them

- separation or rejection is Azazel's specialty—that 'I alone am left' mentality which may or may not be true

- sorcery—in the sense of drugs and spell-binding.

Yet Jesus, as ever, shows us the way forward.

On Yom Kippur, there was a ceremony involving a lamb[100] as well as a ritual involving two goats and the casting of lots. Jesus was not only the scapegoat sent out into the wilderness, He was the lamb that was slain. He combined in His one person, the sacrificial lamb of the Passover and Yom Kippur, as well as the scapegoat and sacrificial goat of Yom Kippur.

In our own lives, we can experience both the pain of being sacrificed by others as well as the wounding that comes from being scapegoated. If we are repeatedly blamed, shamed or asked to bear responsibility for things that have nothing to do with us, ultimately to be cast out—thus symbolically made to carry the sin away—we've been cast in the role of the scapegoat.

When this happens from an early age, when the family dynamic is set up with a designated scapegoat and that's the label stuck to us, it's very difficult to step out of that role and stop accepting blame. We feel guilty for not allowing others to scapegoat us! But the only thing we should feel guilty for is continuing to accept the sin-bearer role that rightly belongs to Jesus! Guilt is our friend in this instance, not rejection: guilt that drives us to Jesus in repentance.

The other side of the coin of the Day of Atonement is becoming the sacrifice. This is just as wrong for us as accepting the position of scapegoat. When, out of our unsanctified pity, we try to bear in our own body or emotions or mind the sufferings of others, we take on burden-bearing way beyond anything the Lord asks of us.

Naturally, there are people who do both—sacrifice themselves and become the scapegoat too. This indicates a double cord of unbelief—one, we have doubts that the atonement of Jesus is all-sufficient and, two, we harbour a deep-seated conviction that, as a consequence, we have to help Him out a little by sacrificing ourselves.

It's true that we have to *make* a sacrifice. But we never have to *be* the sacrifice.

Making a sacrifice is the role of a priest. When Jesus took His disciples to Caesarea Philippi, Simon acquired a new name after he spoke up and confessed Jesus was the Messiah. That new name is, in English, *Peter*; in Greek, *Petros*; in Aramaic, *Kefa*; and in Hebrew, *Cephas*.

It was the same name as that of the high priest at the time, Caiaphas.

Now this was no coincidence. Way back in the distant past, fathers had the right to be priests in their own household. Firstborn sons had the right to be priests for the wider family clan. This privilege was lost at Mount Sinai as a direct consequence of the sin involving the golden calf—and, thereafter, the right to be priests was vested solely in the Levites. The position of high priest was even further restricted: it was the exclusive preserve of the line of Aaron.

Nonetheless, when the kingdom of David split into Judah and Israel, two rival high priests set up camp: in Jerusalem, there was a high priestly line coming from Aaron but, in Dan, just a few minutes' walk down the road from Caesarea Philippi, there was until the Exile a high priestly line descended from Moses.[101]

So when Jesus gave Simon the name of the high priest Caiaphas, He was prophesying that the right to be a priest in your own household was about to return. Now, did He give this right just to Simon Peter? Well, Peter's own words on the stone and the priesthood are recorded in 1 Peter 2:4–10 and there he makes it clear Jesus was talking about everyone.

When Jesus restored the priesthood, it wasn't about a reformation of the line of Aaron or the line of Moses. It was a gift to all believers.

Through covenant with our High Priest Jesus, we become priests of His line—the line of Melchizedek.

Through covenant with the Chief Cornerstone Jesus, we become living stones—built on Him as the foundation.

Through covenant with the Despised and Rejected One, we become empowered to overcome the spirit of rejection.

But this means we need to excise other covenants in our life. My personal experience of rejecting alliances with these spirits is that they don't take 'no' as *no*. At least not permanently *no*. Just *no for now*.

But being specific, saying, 'I renounce and revoke this agreement of my ancestors with rejection and my own complicity with it through dejection; I say 'no' forever to it and I ask Jesus to eject it to the place prepared for it,' is quite different. The spirits are on notice that you mean to do business with Jesus and only Him. And once they're sure of that, they'll move on.

God gives us weapons for the war against Azazel, as well as armour to protect us. He promises to be our paraclete—that is, our battle companion, who covers us by fighting back-to-back with us so that we only have to defend ourselves on one front. The primary weapon God gives us is the fruit of *self-control,* 'egkráteia', *empowerment.*

One of the world's best known longitudinal cohort studies is the Dunedin Study.[102] Begun in the early 1970s, this research initiative has tracked 1037 people[103] born over a span of twelve months in one city in southern New Zealand. Of the many observations to come out of this landmark project, one of the most significant is that the greatest predictor of success in later life is a child's capacity during their early years for self-control, self-discipline or delayed gratification.

Success in the natural comes from self-control. How much more does empowerment to achieve our life's calling comes from realising the limits of our self-control and asking for God's help.

However, this weaponised Fruit is only part of God's strategy for our defence. The armour of God is His additional gift of protection to us. He clothes us in it through His kiss and He also commands us to pray for others to receive it. In a very real sense, it's not so much armour for us as individuals but armour for the entire local body of Christ.

This divine armour is specifically designed for passing over thresholds; it's the sort of heavy-duty protection needed for safely entering into the firestorm that may well explode around us as we step up to our calling. The threshold aspect of its make-up is indicated by the multiple references to parts of a doorway encoded in the Greek text. Each piece of gear is additionally multi-faceted—which is another way of saying they are imbued with aspects of grace. The armour is simultaneously royal robes, priestly garments and a warrior's garb. It's fragrant, it's musical, it's connected to land, it's jewelled, it's dazzling in colour, it's a scroll, it's a kiss!

God's promises of protection and provision for us are not only found described in the Armour of God, but also in Psalm 91. When Jesus was on the threshold of entering into His own calling, He was out in the wilderness, fasting. There the devil came to tempt and test Him. The satan suggested He throw Himself down from the top of the Temple, by quoting this verse as reassurance that God would shield Him from harm:

> *He will command His angels concerning You, and they will lift You up in their hands, so that You will not strike Your foot against a stone.*

> Matthew 4:6 NIV, quoting Psalm 91:12

Now, as we've seen, striking your foot against a stone had special connotations for ancient peoples: it meant refusing covenant. The satan is suggesting to Jesus that God won't break His Word, so it's fine to test His covenantal defence by agreement to a diabolic experiment. The enemy of our souls will twist any assent to His advantage—and quite often we are ignorant of what His designs are.[104] Had Jesus actually jumped, He would have covenanted with the satan.

In a sense, the devil is utilising good rabbinical practice by highlighting this particular verse. A teacher would quote a line from the Scriptures, expecting a student to be able to respond with the next few verses. In this instance, the following line is:

You will tread on the lion and cobra; you will trample the young lion and serpent.

Psalm 91:13 BSB

The satan, I believe, has identified itself throughout the interaction with Jesus as the spirit of Python, but here in my view, it identifies itself as the representative of a coalition of hostile forces. The cobra is 'pethen', *python*, and the young lions, as we have seen, are the brood of the goddess Asherah who was also called *mistress of serpents*, while the 'serpent' at the end of the verse is 'tannin' or *sea monster*, probably indicating Leviathan.

Earlier in the psalm, however, translators have encoded a subtle reference to Pan. God promises us that if we make Him our refuge, then we will have no cause to fear *'the pestilence that walks in darkness, nor... the destruction that lays waste at noonday.'* (Psalm 91:6 NKJV)

I would never have guessed this until I was reading *The Roadmender* by Michael Fairless,[105] a mega-bestseller of the first decade of the twentieth century. It was lovely and lyrical and hopeful, but it kept making obscure allusions that the author obviously expected the reader to understand. I've found that, when this occurs, it's almost always an indicator of common cultural knowledge. The author assumes she doesn't have to explain because she believes she doesn't have to; after all, everyone *knows*. Now one of these obscure statements mentioned Pan and 'white cliffs'.

I was baffled. I thought of all those photographs I've seen of Caesarea Philippi and I couldn't imagine anyone thinking those cliffs were anything other than red. Ok, maybe pink. Maybe brown. White? Not a chance.

I wondered what the 'white cliffs' was about. Eventually I finally found what I was looking for in *The Greek Islands* by Lawrence Durrell. There, in a discussion of the white cliffs of Lefkas and their association with Pan, he says: '...the noontide is his hour. Theocritus writes: "Nay, shepherd, it must not be; ye must not pipe at noon for fear of Pan."' He then goes on to say that Pan was active enough to influence the Greek translators of Psalm 91 who obliquely referenced him as the *'destruction that wastes at noonday.'*

There are many subtle aspects of Psalm 91, but the one that eludes so many readers, including those who recite it every day as protection for themselves and their families, is that it's *conditional.*

> *If you say, 'The Lord is my refuge,' and you make the Most High your dwelling, no harm will overtake you, no disaster will come near your tent.*

Psalm 91:9–10 NIV

That little word *'if'* is so often overlooked. It's implied throughout the psalm: yet, in our culture, we think that saying alone is enough, but speech and action was never separated in Hebrew thought. To say one thing and then do otherwise was to practise hypocrisy. But, in today's church, we think: if I say the Lord is my refuge, then it is so. After all, I speak out my reality.

No. We need to stop deluding ourselves. If we have a false refuge that is still intact and remains our stronghold of defence in times of trouble, then the Lord is simply not our refuge. We're deceiving ourselves. It doesn't matter how many times we recite Psalm 91 over our lives. Python, Leviathan, Azazel—as well as the other threshold guardians who may be hidden under obscure allusions—have legal rights to attack us if we've still got false refuges and the unholy alliances that go with them.

Psalm 91 is about the protection available to us as we cross over the threshold into our calling. However that availability is dependent on making the Lord our refuge, not holding on to the coping mechanisms we've found so useful.

Prayer

Abba Father, may Your name be kept holy as I speak.

Let me start with an apology. There have been times when I've been thrust into the role of scapegoat. I've accepted it even while fighting it, I've been cancelled and sent away but I've come back for more, I've hidden away while making up speeches in my head to combat it— words I knew I would never dare deliver—and I've found myself a hundred coping mechanisms. Yes, I eventually realised I could take the rejection to Jesus and sit with Him. But I still need to apologise for usurping Him, for taking His role as the Scapegoat. Sure I was pressured into it and I didn't want it, but it happened anyway. Lord Jesus, I'm sorry I was complicit with others, even to the smallest degree, in trying to push You out of Your rightful place.

Let me continue with an apology for the times I've scapegoated others or been part of the scapegoating of others. Forgive me for believing one side of a story without making the slightest effort to discover the other side, let alone Your views on the matter.

Abba, I repent of taking on the role of the scapegoat for others and I repent of participating in the scapegoating of others. Forgive me, Lord, for my agreement with the spirit of religion, since scapegoating is integral to separation, sacrifice and sorcery. I renounce that agreement, Father, and I ask Jesus to both forgive me as well as grant my words the empowering grace to become true vehicles of repentance, renunciation and reconciliation with You.

Father, as well as scapegoating, there has been robbery. The spirit of fear has created much chaos in my life that I've grumbled behind the scenes but been unwilling to confront the thieves. So often the good I have achieved with much effort has been scattered. Sometimes my work has been attributed to another and they have received the reward due to me. Privately they've admitted that they usurped my place. I sometimes wondered if I wore a badge that said, *'Ignore me'* or *'Reject me'* but I now realise that I have, in part, simply been reaping what I have sown.

I invited a spirit of fear and rejection to be my constant companion and that spirit accepted my invitation. He displaced You as the quiet centre-point of my life. To keep his position, he made sure that I was overlooked and rejected and that my faith in You was defiled by dishonour. Father, forgive me, because I did not know what I was doing.

In the name of Jesus Christ of Nazareth who is the spirit of love, peace and joy, I repent of my foolish invitation and ask You, through the cross of Jesus, to cancel and rescind it. Thank You, Father, for Your forgiveness. I resolve by Your grace and the empowerment of the blood of Jesus that, from this day forward, I will act in accordance with Your will.

Thank You, Jesus, for Your faithfulness, mercy, love and goodness in making it possible for me to return home to the Father. Thank You for being the Lamb slain before the foundation of the world and the Scapegoat all-sufficient to carry away the sins of the world.

In Your Name. Amen.

7

The Art of Story

I'D LIKE TO FINISH WITH THREE STORIES, all of them true. One is about a lamb, one about a goat and one about some students who taught me a lesson about rejection.

I'd come back to the classroom after several years away from teaching. That meant I had to be re-certified through a series of weekly in-class inspections. Because I was having so much trouble with my Year 9 German class, I invited the deputy principal to come and advise me on what I could do to improve. I thought it was an efficient plan: have an inspection and get some assistance at the same time. For ten weeks, the deputy principal watched every lesson descend into a shambling chaos and finally he said: 'I'm sorry but I'm going to have to fail you. But before your accreditation is cancelled, I'd like to give you another chance. Let me see your best class.'

So I invited him to observe my Year 10 Science class the next day. As he arrived, I noticed his expression turn to surprise. He greeted about a dozen students by name, a feat which was to my mind very impressive, given the school had over 1700 pupils. I didn't realise the significance of his knowledge until later that day. The students were their usual well-behaved selves and the lesson got off to a flying start. After only ten minutes, the deputy stood up and whispered to me on his way out, 'I've seen enough. Come to my office as soon as the lesson is done.'

My heart sank. My teaching career was apparently over. As soon as I arrived in his office, the deputy asked, 'That was your *best* class?'

I nodded.

He looked at me incredulously. 'That class has a dozen of the worst terrors in the entire school. Whose crazy idea was it to put them all together in one place? But they were eating out of the palm of your hand! You're a good teacher! I don't know what is going on in that German class of yours, but there must be some hidden dynamic that is totally toxic.'

Toxic seriously underrated the situation. In other classes, these students were individually like Dr Jekyll, but the moment they gathered together for German, a collective Mr Hyde emerged. You may wonder that I'm describing this class like a single organism, but that's genuinely what it was. For some reason I never fathomed, they acted as a completely unified pack—and if there was an alpha in the mix, no one ever discerned him or her.

I battled on through the rest of the school year—vainly trying to control the rebellion and anarchy. I hated the class and they hated me. And when the end of the year finally, blessedly, arrived, we threw each other a party. It was the only thing we'd mutually agreed on all year— we were so deliriously happy at the thought of never ever having to endure another moment of each other's company that it was time for a celebration. Recognising we were about to part ways forever and were better off without each other, we wanted to make our last time together a happy one before moving on. We even invited the deputy principal to our farewell.

One student who, not surprisingly, flunked German but was nevertheless such a superb cyclist he starred at the Olympics just a few years after this, asked the deputy, 'Can I throw a cream pie at you, sir?'

I signalled frantically for the deputy to indicate 'no' but he ignored me, thinking the student was joking. 'Sure!' he laughed. Not even a second later, a cream pie caught him on the chin, splattered his hair and dribbled down his shirt. How could he discipline the student? After all, the boy had asked permission.

So with that, it was all over. Except... well, God had other ideas.

The holidays came and went. A new school year started and, five weeks in, the deputy principal unexpectedly turned up at the door of one of my classes. 'You know what this is about, don't you?' he asked.

Words to strike sheer terror into your heart as you try to imagine what you might possibly have done that led to a death, maiming or other traumatic accident. 'No.'

'You're losing this class,' he informed me. 'You'll be taking over the third German class in Year 10.'

I frowned, trying to recall which teacher I'd be replacing. *Wait*, I thought, *there are only two German classes at that level: advanced and ordinary.* 'There isn't a third German class in Year 10.'

'There is now. You're the only one who can handle them.'

Suddenly the tone of his words registered. The meaning hit me.

'*What?!*' I squealed. '*No!* You can't mean this. You nearly refused my certification because of them!'

'You're the only one who can handle them.'

'How can you say that? You saw the chaos!'

'You're the only one who can handle them.'

'That's insane! Have you forgotten the cream pie?'

'You're the only one who can handle them.'

I went home that night so depressed I seriously considered resigning. I prayed in desperation, trying to discern if God was telling me to quit teaching. The next day, the deputy escorted the class to my room. They came up the corridor, scowling and sullen, jostling each other.

And then they saw me.

Realising what was happening, they broke into radiant smiles. Seeing those beaming faces, I decided I was doomed. The deputy handed them each a new timetable and left us together. He'd made it clear I wasn't expected to teach them, just babysit.

Yet, to my amazement, the smiles weren't because they were planning devilish mayhem. They were actually ecstatic to see me. As the lesson progressed, they behaved well. No, 'well' doesn't cut it. They were *perfect.* And over the next weeks and months, their changed attitude remained. They were friendly, cooperative, courteous, considerate, willing to learn. They acted with a maturity and civility beyond their years. My horror class had become a dream. I *loved* teaching them. Eventually the opportunity arose to ask: 'You remember last year? Why the change?'

'Miss,' they said, 'that other class was a nightmare. The teacher didn't care about us. She hated us—she'd send us to detention before we did anything wrong. Before we even got into the classroom. But the detention room refused to take us. So we spent three weeks, sitting in the courtyard outside the deputy principal's office, because no one would give us a chance.'

'C'mon, guys,' I said. 'That's a harsh assessment. Remember last year? Mutual loathing. I hated you, you hated me.'

'No, Miss.' There was universal shaking of heads. 'You do not rate when it comes to hating. You don't know what we've been through. We weren't given any work when we were in the deputy's courtyard, so we had a lot of time to think. And we realised you never rejected us. You never stopped trying to teach us. That other teacher did after just a couple of days. She didn't care. She was totally indifferent. She didn't treat us as human.'

Theirs was a very different perception to that of the teacher who, as one of the most high-profile professing Christians in a state school, saw herself simply as a firm disciplinarian. For the greater good of all the students in her class, she'd installed hard boundaries to deal with a gang of inveterate disruptors. But that gang saw her as uncaring, indifferent and rejecting. They knew that, even if they were welcomed back to class, they'd be so far behind they could never catch up. In their view, this was all about breaking their wills and shaming them indefinitely.

Terrie Coleman says: 'Indifference is the worst form of rejection.' She's right. That's what this class taught me. Sustained indifference is in a category of its own when it comes to rejection. It's said people would prefer to be abused rather than ignored.

This story could so easily have turned out differently. By the end of the year, most of the students scraped a pass in German and a couple of them, against my advice, even signed up for the only German language class in the senior school.

We overcome the spirit of rejection by sitting and watching for six days with Jesus and beginning the process of self-control. Although these students didn't sit in the courtyard with Jesus, they did have a lot of time to reflect. It turns out that even fleshly self-control has its place. Because, at the end of the day, self-control was the only way out of their dilemma, yet they weren't willing to exercise it with anyone who'd rejected them. Their coping mechanism was to fight to the death.

But when they looked back on the previous year, particularly on the last interaction we'd had—the farewell party—they came to recognise a subtle truth. Rejection is not the same as acknowledging that we simply can't get on together.

Even as we recognise that we're so very different a clash is inevitable, we can still respect each other enough to try to discover ways to minimise conflict. After all, maybe we've mistaken rebellion for what we really want: independence. And that does not mean terminating the relationship because, as we've already noted, independence is a bilateral negotiation. Rebellion is a unilateral declaration.

This is the last of Azazel's agenda: to incite rebellion. It was, after all, a leader of an angelic mutiny. Naturally he wants to counterfeit the work of God and remake his adherents—and those he claims as his adherents—in his own image. Yet that will drive us into becoming rebels and traitors against God.

Sometimes we are tempted to rebel, and sometimes we tempt others to rebel. Our unwillingness to listen and negotiate often pushes people, particularly teenagers, from a legitimate desire for independence into overt rebellion. Long before cancel culture became so strident in refusing to listen to any point of view other than its own, many leaders practised the art of tempting others to rebellion by their indifference. Such leadership is in league with Azazel and is as much in need of repentance as those who fall into rebellion. A pre-emptive strike—like the teacher who tried to break the will of the students by sending them to detention before they did anything wrong—punishes people for *being*, not for *misbehaviour*.

A true bilateral negotiation doesn't break anyone's will. It does not introduce shame or manipulation; it discovers strengths and weaknesses and how to work together to achieve what it impossible separately. It values others as divine image-bearers, as *'labourers together with God'* (1 Corinthians 3:9 KJV) and as covenant partners with Jesus.

It's time to break our covenants with Azazel and turn to God.

A bruised reed He will not break, and a smoldering wick He will not snuff out, till He has brought justice through to victory.

Matthew 12:20 NIV

There are several words for 'reeds' in Hebrew—one is connected to thresholds[106] and one to brothers. The students in my German class became convinced that they were subjective to pre-emptive discipline in order to bring about broken wills and indefinite shame.

God does not want to break our will—He wants us to surrender it so He can strengthen it and empower us with self-control. The breaking of will is not a tactic of Azazel, but rather of its close ally, the spirit of abuse. Still these powers often work together for obvious reasons.

Occasionally a ewe will reject a lamb. She may not have enough milk, or she may be ill. She may have discerned a defect in the lamb that will make it difficult for it to thrive. If the lamb is returned to the mother for feeding, the ewe will kick it or butt it until it goes away. The mother's decision is final. Once this happens, she won't change her mind. The rejected lamb hangs its head low in dejection, like a scrap of torn wool. Its spirit has been broken.

Repeated abuse and rejection do not empower us towards self-control; they endeavour to break our will so we can be more easily controlled by others. Those students in my German class who were concerned about being crushed into powerlessness and then coerced by shame were right on the money.

These baby sheep with broken spirits are called 'bummer lambs'. No other mother will accept them. Unless the shepherd takes them in hand, they will die of starvation. They need to be bottle-fed until they are strong enough to go back to the flock and graze on pasture by themselves. Bummer lambs of course become deeply attached to the shepherd and, when the flock is called, they're the first to run to the shepherd's voice.

Many of us are like these lambs—rejected and abandoned. Our wills are broken, we suffer separation anxiety. We need more than nurture, we need to snuggle into the Shepherd's arms and listen to His heartbeat.

There is no question that staying in the embrace of the Lord is hard—especially when we realise that we're with Him in Gethsemane, *the oil press*. And that we have to watch with Him for much more than an hour. It's not a matter of asking Him to rebuke the spirit of rejection and elbowing it out of our lives forevermore. It's a matter of abiding with the Rejected One in the place of pressing and crushing until He's brought our wills into alignment with His and empowered us to self-control through that placement. Yet every moment of that abiding and that alignment requires His empowerment. Our 'self'-control is His enabling power.

Gethsemane, *the oil press*, was where the sins of the world were pressed on to Jesus. It should remind us of the ritual on the Day of Atonement. Besides the scapegoat ritual, there was one involving a lamb which was tied to the altar and inspected to see if it was flawless. Then the High Priest pressed the lamb to place upon it the sins of the people. Then the lamb was slain and at 3 o'clock, the high priest shouted, 'It is finished!'

When we sit in Gethsemane with Jesus, we're not going there to participate in the atonement. That's an easy error to make when we've spent our lives being scapegoated. We're there to hand over our status as scapegoat and to acknowledge that we've been manipulated into accepting a position that was never meant to be ours. Some people need to hand over the throne of their lives to Jesus. Others need to hand over the role of their lives to Jesus so that it can be redeemed.

But what does that look like? The answer, not surprisingly, lies in the natural world of goat-keeping. Many farmers who otherwise intensely dislike these animals often kept them anyway because they had one particular prized ability. The spirit of the scapegoat might specialise in fomenting panic, but goats themselves do not panic in fires. Consequently, farmers would often keep one in the barn with other animals, particularly horses, to lead them to safety in the event of a fire.[107]

If you've been cast in the role of scapegoat all your life, ask Jesus to redeem that typecasting so you can help people who are panicking overcome their fears. Be the one who, when the enemy fires his flaming arrows and sets the world ablaze, points the way forward and out. When those around you don't know which way to turn because fear has taken such a deep hold on their souls, be the one who speaks courage and confidence.

God has not given us a spirit of fear, but of power, love, and self-control.

2 Timothy 1:7 BSB

That spirit of fear[108] is countered by the power, love and self-control Jesus offers us.

During the Troubles in Northern Ireland, walls of separation up to eight metres high were built in cities like Belfast, Derry, Lurgan and Portadown. These barriers topped by high wire were called Peace Lines and were constructed to minimise violent interactions between Catholic and Protestant neighbourhoods. In West Belfast, one of the Peace Lines divided The Shankill from The Falls.[109] There, on Springfield Road, the Cornerstone Community brought the members of different faiths together to pray, talk and share their lives. This small interdenominational group created an urban farm on one side of the Peace Line and invited volunteers from both sides of the wall to come and care for the animals. Then they bought a field on the far side of the wall and put a goat in it. And so the volunteers could care for the goat, they constructed a gate in the wall.[110]

The Peace Line, paradoxically, promoted peace through dividing neighbours. The Cornerstone Community promoted it through a gate in the wall between The Shankill, *old church*, and The Falls, *enclosures*.

We started with the question: *what should we do about the goat?*

We find the answer in this imagery from Belfast: a **goat**, **Cornerstone**, a **gate**, old **church**, **enclosure**, factions allegedly at **war over faith** and **spirituality**.

Look too at this imagery from Caesarea Philippi: at an **enclosure** dedicated to a **goat**-godling, Jesus gave Simon a name meaning **cornerstone** and proclaimed the beginning of His **church**, saying that the **gates** of hell would not prevail against it, thereby effectively announcing a **war against the faith and spirituality** of that age.

The same things manifested themselves thousands of years apart—and so we can identify the same spirit pushing its agenda in our own era. And we can also see this spirit being overcome once again.

The advancement of the kingdom of God comes about through Jesus who is our Peace and who has broken down the dividing walls of hostility between us. He is the Cornerstone who was rejected, He is the Scapegoat and the Lamb that was slain before the foundation of the world. He is the War Messiah who walked into the council of the seventy young lions and proclaimed their rule of the nations to be over. He calls on us, as His church, bring a new government to the world and to war against the influence of the spiritual forces of wickedness with love, joy, peace, patience, kindness, goodness, faithfulness, gentleness and self-control.

Remember the agenda of the spirit of fear as it hunts you? It's not just to push you into panic and destructive choices, and it's not just to drive you towards diving into a hole that you'll fit out as a false refuge. It's also to follow after you and undo the good that you do.

But that is not what God wants.

> *Your light will break forth like the dawn, and your healing will quickly appear; then your righteousness will go before you, and the glory of the Lord will be your rear guard.*

Isaiah 58:8 NIV

He wants goodness and mercy to follow after you. He wants His glory to be your rearguard. He wants His kiss to armour you and His peace to watch over you and His empowering 'self'-control to keep you. These are the promises He makes to those He summons by name and invites to pass over the threshold into their calling.

Sit with Jesus.

And allow Him, as the rejected Cornerstone, to show you how to master the spirit of rejection.

Prayer

Our Father in heaven:

Hallowed be Your Name. May it be blessed, honoured and glorified in all that I do and say.

May Your kingdom come. May it not be undone. Rebuke the evil one following after me to uproot the good that I do to advance Your kingdom. Command goodness and kindness to follow me all the days of my life and, just occasionally, overtake me.

May Your will be done on earth as it is in heaven. Frustrate those who work against Your will and bring down their plans. Show Yourself strong on the earth through exposing the deeds of darkness. Shine Your Light on the truth, cause faithfulness to spring up and justice to pour down from heaven, and righteousness and peace to kiss each other.

Give us this day our daily bread. Provide again the blessing of food and of Your Word and allow each to bless and nourish us. Create in us a hunger for You, the Bread of life and the Cup of eternal salvation.

And forgive us our debts, as we also have forgiven our debtors. Empower our wills, Father, to forgive.

Strengthen us with Your grace to be Your agents of love in the world.

And lead us not into temptation, but deliver us from the evil one. In the time of trial, when we sense fear and rejection, and feel panic arising within us, lead us away from our false refuge and draw us to Yourself. Deliver us from the spirit of rejection by teaching us to master it through the empowerment Jesus offers us.

For Yours is the kingdom and the power and the glory, forever. Amen.

Yes and amen.

Appendix 1

Summary

Rejection is a fact of life.

There is a spirit of rejection identified in this book by the primary names Pan and Azazel. This spirit can latch onto your fleshly feelings and cause you to choose a number of options that don't involve sitting with Jesus the rejected Cornerstone and genuinely sorting out the matter.

These options include reacting to people who reject us by:

- fighting
- freezing
- fleeing
- flattering
- forestalling
- forgetting

The spirit of rejection is not particular about your response. It is indifferent to your freezing in fright or moving to fight or rushing to flight.

Just so long as you don't hold up your hand and tug at the tassels of Love's mantle—just so long as you don't touch the hem of Jesus' prayer shawl—just so long as you don't sit with Him in the rejection. Anything but that. Anything but surrender our fleshly coping mechanisms, face our fear of true rejection and simply stay with Him.

This spirit often whispers kindly that it's our only friend—convincing us that 'I alone am left.' In fact, it functions by hunting us. It wants the hunt to cause us to panic and make irrational decisions. In particular, it wants these irrational decisions to include covenants with it or one of its allies.

This ally may be the spirit of wishing or any other spirit tasked with barring our way into our calling.

The spirit of rejection wants us to become so sensitive that it doesn't even need to provoke panic in us. It wants us so finely attuned that we sense the approach of rejection and automatically head off on the well-worn track leading to our false refuge. It wants us to become a little more comfortable there, it wants the pathway to be a little smoother and more direct each time; it wants the habit to become more instinctive and less a matter of conscious volition. It doesn't want us thinking and deliberately *choosing*,[111] it wants us reacting robotically.

Now every false refuge contains idols. That's their nature. And every one of the threshold spirits want us bound by agreements with these idols. The spirit of rejection doesn't simply tempt us to enter a false refuge, it hunts us so that we race there for safety.

But, as part of its hunt, this spirit has a secondary agenda: it follows after us to undo the good that we do and to destroy the Kingdom-works that we build.

Its wider agenda and tactics include:

- **rejection and marginalisation**
- **provoking panic and fear**
- **inducing a sense of being hunted**
- **lust and promotion of lust**
- **creating division and igniting war**
- **inciting rebellion**
- **tempting us to rely on our own strength**
- **undoing the good that we do**
- **drawing us into false religion, characterised by sacrifice, separation and sorcery**
- **scapegoating**

Azazel was listed in the Book of Enoch as one of the leaders of the Watchers—sometimes as the supreme leader, sometimes as the commander of a smaller group. He allegedly taught humanity the arts of metallurgy and weaponry, as well as cosmetic-making—the latter not only a means of fending off rejection but also of promoting lust. He *may* also be known as Samyaza, and have additionally taught root-cutting and spell-binding. This combination of knowledge—drug-formulation and incantation—was anciently called pharmakeia, *sorcery*. Azazel is mentioned in Scripture in the ritual for Yom Kippur, the Day of Atonement, in reference to the scapegoat sent out into the wilderness carrying the sins of the people on its head.

Pan was a goat deity, worshipped by the Greeks. He had a ritual cult centre at Caesarea Philippi where Simon identified Jesus as the Messiah and received the name Cephas, meaning *cornerstone*. The symbolism of this interaction on the Day of Atonement indicates that Jesus identified Pan as Azazel. The word 'panic' derives from the name Pan.

Pan's wild hunt is replicated in many cultures. From Celtic culture, Bran 'the wonderful Head' seems to be the hunter who follows behind you to undo the good that you do.

The primary weapon to overcome Azazel is self-control: this is to be understood as empowerment by Jesus to stand in the face of terror. This has the additional advantage of preparing us to obey God's Terror who can sweep our enemies before us, providing we obey his commands. This angel bears the name, War. God's answer to the warcraft of Pan and Azazel is this 'Hornet' who specialises in strategy and battle.

God also gives us armour for the battle to be received through His kiss.

Mastery of the spirit of rejection is not the same as casting out rejection itself. If we were able to cast out rejection, we would no longer identify with one of the most significant character qualities of Jesus as the Rejected Cornerstone and Suffering Servant.

We learn to overcome this spirit by sitting with Jesus in rejection, as we would if we were watching with Him in Gethsemane. In theory this should take six days, in practice, it may take longer because we may uncover other spirits or hindrances in the process.

It is wise to ask God to rebuke this spirit for following us and undoing the good we do, tearing down our attainments for His kingdom and transforming our legacy into ashes. Instead we should ask for Goodness and Mercy to follow us, and for the Glory of the Lord to be our rearguard.

God wants us to heal history—this includes our personal history, the history of our family and beyond that, our town, our nation and our world. He wants us to work together to do it. To stop rejecting one another but, even if we can't stand one another—like I couldn't stand that German class—to find a way to work together.

To do what it takes. To be persistent. Not in a fleshly way, but in spending time with Jesus the rejected Cornerstone and asking Him how to fix the situation. After all, it's what He does best.

Appendix 2

The First Disciple

The first follower of Jesus was Andrew. Along with another unnamed disciple—most probably John—he heard Jesus called, *'the Lamb of God'* by John the Baptist and went after Him. (John 1:36–37)

Throughout the Gospels, Andrew is the one who brings others to Jesus. They follow him to find Jesus. He's the one who brings his brother, Simon Peter, to Jesus. He's the one who brings the boy with the five loaves and two fish to Jesus. He's the one who, together with Philip, brings the Greek inquirers to Jesus.

This is the most prominent characteristic of the apostle Andrew.

His name is from the Greek, Andreas, and it means *manly.*

But let's pretend the name is not Greek. Let's look at some wordplay across languages. Many people realise that hostile spirits are extreme legalists, but it's easy to overlook their flip side as gamesters. For them, it's not just about the meaning of words but about how that meaning can be folded, spindled, twisted and even mocked, thus parodying the Word Himself.

So, let's pretend 'Andrew' is from the north, not the south, of Europe and that the sounds that make up the word could hide a meaning other than the name of the first disciple. 'And-' might well come from 'ander' mean *other* or *stranger*, while '-drew', sounds like 'dru', *oak* or *tree*. This could even point to the druids, *those who know the oak tree*.

My suspicion is that Andrew became the patron saint of Scotland because there was an inherent ambiguity in the name. By it, the Celtic worshippers of Christ could point to Andrew, His first disciple, the one who was constantly leading those following him to His master. But other worshippers, those who wished to conceal their true allegiance, could think to themselves that they were really paying homage to the *'other tree'.* Quite a few godlings could be masked under such a name, but I think the primary one was Bran, whose symbol was the alder tree, the raven and the head. Yet he is the one who follows after us to undo the good we do.

This 'follower' aspect sets Bran up as the exact opposite of Saint Andrew. Bran became the national protector of Britain in ancient folklore. The tapestry of legend is chopped into different quilt pieces and made to fit different beds in different regions across England, Wales, Scotland and Ireland, however, I believe that Bran the Blessed can also be identified in various stories as The Dagda (pronounced *'day'*), Urbgen, Urien Rheged,

Uther Ben, Ysbadden, Giant Hawthorn, The Raven King and the Wonderful Head.

As I point out in many of my books, I believe most parents name their children for the unresolved issues of their family line. If that issue is rejection, the following names are usually prominent for those of western heritage: Brian, Bronwyn, Brown, Byron, Byrne, Burns, Björn, Bryant (in fact, just about any European name starting with B, especially BR), Andrew and Anderson and their variants.

The connection between Pan and Bran in the world of legend is tenuous at best. However, in the realm of enemy spirits, the subversion of words is a constant pastime. Words need to retain sufficient of their old meaning to become vehicles of deception, yet also have already been twisted so that their new meaning holds sway in any legal challenge. Thus, I believe the connection between Pan and Bran slides through the Celtic word 'pen' meaning *head*. It can also be attached to mountain summits and headlands, chieftains and the sources of rivers.

This means that we can add to our list of names above that indicate a possible covenant in a family with the spirit of rejection: Conn, Ken, Kenneth, Kennedy, Kieran, Ross, Rose, Roslyn, Robyn, Penny, Pansy and sometimes Patrick along with their variants.

We need to consult with the Holy Spirit to check if such a covenant has ever been raised. It is rare for a covenant to be ratified in our own generation, largely because we no longer know what actually constitutes a genuine covenant. However, it is exceedingly common for us to be complicit with the agreements of the past through our own beliefs, attitudes and actions. We are not responsible for the raising of the covenant, but we are responsible for it continuing on into the future.

If the Holy Spirit indicates this is the case, then in addition to any other covenant still operating in the family line, a name covenant with the spirit of rejection will need to be severed—particularly for those people who bear a name that hints of ambiguous loyalty.

Appendix 3

With Jesus for 6 Days

If you choose to spend time with Jesus for six days in order to master the spirit of rejection—even if that six days turns out to be broken because of matters He highlights that need to be attended to—you may like to record the testimony that comes out of this time on the following pages.

It is through the Blood of the Lamb and the word of our testimony that we overcome the Accuser. (Revelation 12:11)

Day 1

Reflection Scripture:

> *Jesus went with them to the olive grove called Gethsemane, and He said, 'Sit here while I go over there to pray.'*

Matthew 26:36 NLT

What I said to Jesus

_____

_____

_____

_____

_____

_____

What Jesus said to me

_____

_____

_____

_____

_____

_____

_____

_____

_____

Day 2

Reflection Scripture:

> One day as Jesus was praying in private and the disciples were with Him, He questioned them: 'Who do the crowds say I am?'
>
> They replied, 'Some say John the Baptist; others say Elijah; and still others, that a prophet of old has arisen.'
>
> 'But what about you?' Jesus asked. 'Who do you say I am?'
>
> Peter answered, 'The Christ of God.'

Luke 8:18–20 BSB

What I said to Jesus

_____

_____

_____

_____

_____

What Jesus said to me

_____

_____

_____

_____

_____

_____

_____

_____

Day 3

Reflection Scripture:

> *Then He began to teach them that the Son of Man must suffer many things and be rejected by the elders, chief priests, and scribes, and that He must be killed and after three days rise again. He spoke this message quite frankly, and Peter took Him aside and began to rebuke Him.*
>
> *But Jesus, turning and looking at His disciples, rebuked Peter and said, 'Get behind Me, Satan! For you do not have in mind the things of God, but the things of men.'*

Mark 8:31–33 BSB

What I said to Jesus

_____

_____

_____

_____

What Jesus said to me

_____

_____

_____

_____

_____

_____

_____

Day 4

Reflection Scripture:

After six days Jesus took with Him Peter, James, and John the brother of James, and led them up a high mountain by themselves. There He was transfigured before them. His face shone like the sun, and His clothes became as white as the light.

Suddenly Moses and Elijah appeared before them, talking with Jesus. Peter said to Jesus, 'Lord, it is good for us to be here. If You wish, I will put up three shelters— one for You, one for Moses, and one for Elijah.'

While Peter was still speaking, a bright cloud enveloped them, and a voice from the cloud said, 'This is My beloved Son, in whom I am well pleased. Listen to Him!' When the disciples heard this, they fell facedown in terror.

Then Jesus came over and touched them. 'Get up,' He said. 'Do not be afraid.' And when they looked up, they saw no one except Jesus.

Matthew 17:1–8 BSB

What I said to Jesus

_____

_____

_____

_____

What Jesus said to me

_____

_____

_____

_____

Day 5

Reflection Scripture:

> *We were eyewitnesses of His majesty. For He received honour and glory from God the Father when the voice came to Him from the Majestic Glory, saying, 'This is My beloved Son, in whom I am well pleased.' And we ourselves heard this voice from heaven when we were with Him on the holy mountain.*

2 Peter 1:16–18 BSB

What I said to Jesus

What Jesus said to me

Day 6

What I said to Jesus

What Jesus said to me

Endnotes

1. One of my favourite stories on this theme is at speculativefaith.lorehaven.com/when-dreams-go-to-sleep-the-story-of-stormrise/ (accessed 12 April 2019)

2. Many people are of the theological view that the Cross did away with all legal rights of the enemy and therefore to suggest that the satan has legal rights is false. I do not entirely agree, both because of the testimony of Scripture and my own experience in prayer ministry with many hundreds of people.

   My view is that Jesus, through His death on the Cross, signed the papers to annul the spiritual legal rights of all the powers of darkness. Everything is ready—all the work is done. *It is indeed finished!* The papers only need our co-signature. God does not force us to countersign, nor does He stamp the papers automatically—this would be to violate the very freedom He is offering us through calling us to confess (that is, come into agreement) that we have sinned, that we repent and we want to reconcile and renew relationship with Him. Covenant must not be coerced but a free will decision.

3. In his description of the Armour of God in Ephesians 6, Paul refers to *principalities, powers* and *world-rulers*. Since different English translations are not consistent in the naming of this hierarchy, particularly with regard to the 'powers', please note that I believe the threshold guardians belong to the middle-ranked 'exousia'. Principalities hold sway over cities, regions and nations; powers ('exousia') over the boundaries between cities, regions and nations as well as boundaries of time and state; world-rulers, as their name implies, over worlds.

4. This is based on Acts 16:16 where Paul and Silas encounter the spirit of Python, which many translations render as a 'spirit of divination'.

5. Some, like Leviathan, even adopt different names for those faces—such as Resheph. (See *Dealing with Resheph: Spirit of Trouble*, the previous book in this series.) Of course, in different cultures, the same entity may have a different name.

6. For more details, see *Dealing with Python: Spirit of Constriction*, the first book in this series. It should be pointed out that, when Jesus was tested by Python in the wilderness, He did not bind it. He allowed the test to proceed. When He became aware that the satan had asked to 'sift' Peter like wheat (that is, *test to the point of overthrow*), did He bind the spirit? No, He prayed for a specific outcome for Peter.

7. Job 41:8

8. Thanks to Dr Colin Webster for this definition.

9. Isaiah 1:18 NKJV

10. See *Hidden in the Cleft: True and False Refuge*, the fourth book in this series.

11. For more on name covenants, see either *God's Poetry: The Identity and Destiny Encoded in Your Name* or *Name Covenant: Invitation to Friendship*, the third book in this series.

12. The name 'Pan' was thought by the Romans to mean all, but it is a Greek name and more likely to originate in 'pa', *guardian of the flocks*.

13. He was returning from Zarephath on the coast between Tyre and Sidon where he'd been staying with a widow and her son.

14. Names are so important in Scripture, including the rhyming aspect of them that we should not overlook the appearance of a word close to 'Ziz', spirit of forgetting within the name 'Azazel'. The spelling is different but there is close poetic assonance and, in addition, 'ziz' is connected with the movement of herds. Azazel's alter ego, Pan, *guardian of the flocks*, is also connected with herd movement, especially panicked flight.

15. 1 Kings 20:15

16. Judges 11:1–40. See *Dealing with Resheph: Spirit of Trouble*, the previous book in this series, for further insight into Jesus' lengthy sojourn in Gilead.

17. John 6:32

18. Because ancient Hebrew has no vowels, the word may in fact be 'mizeh', *that which is*, an assertion rather than a question.

19. It is described as a 'nachash', the same kind of fiery serpent that tempted Eve in the Garden of Eden. Leviathan is also described as 'nachash'.

20. The five instances of equivocation—all of which amount to 'no', even if some are not explicit—are as follows:

    • 'Who am I that I should go to Pharaoh...?' he asked. Exodus 3:11

    • 'Suppose I go... what should I say?' Exodus 3:13

    • 'What if they do not believe me or listen to my voice?' Exodus 4:1

    • 'Please, Lord... I have never been eloquent... I am slow of speech and tongue.' Exodus 4:10

    • 'Please, Lord, send someone else.' Exodus 4:13

21. Exodus 4:24

22. There are two technical terms for 'making' a covenant used in Scripture: you can *cut* a covenant or *raise* a covenant. *Cutting* a covenant is the more common term.

23. This word for *reed*, 'suph', derives from a word for *to come to an end* or *to cease* or *to be fulfilled*. Reeds, in marking a transitional space between land and water show the point at which dry land ceases or comes to an end. Also related is 'suphah', *storm wind*, perhaps from the notion of storms ending a period of dry weather.

24. The word for *threshold*, 'saph', derives from a word for *basin* or *goblet*, referring to the shallow receptacle carved into the cornerstone which caught the blood dripping from the lintel. The difference in spelling between 'suph' and 'saph' is simply the lack of a central 'vav' in 'saph'.

25. See *God's Pageantry* for details about how the names of the first four spirits listed here are encoded in the landscape of the Exodus journey.

26. A threshold word—the Hebrew spelling of sapphire actually contains 'saph', the word for *threshold*. In addition, the use of sapphire here during a banquet which is also threshold covenant ceremony reinforces the overtones of the event as a rite in which mutual defence is understood.

27. This conflict in messaging that was part of the earliest experiences of Moses as a baby would have been reinforced at the lodging in the wilderness where God tried to kill him. The trauma of a threat of death was written—epigenetically—into the DNA of Moses and would have a devastating outcome in the life of his grandson Jonathan.

28. *'This'* mountain is not some abstract concept of a high peak; it is in fact Mount Hermon. Since Hermon was considered to be the Mount of Assembly for the principalities of the nations, I believe that Jesus was possibly saying that it is not so much the physical mountain that will be removed, but instead what the mountain represents in the spiritual world will be. Have the faith of a mustard seed and then not one of the angel guardians of the nations will be able to stand in your way. In other words, those who believe in Jesus are called to do better than Elijah—and to face up to these principalities and defeat them. The 'mustard seed' of faith required is simply sufficient trust in Jesus to reach for the hem of His prayer shawl and join our faith to His. It is His faith that does all the heavy lifting to move the mountain, not ours.

29. Some commentators, who don't believe in demons, are convinced that Jesus 'fitted' His healings to the prevailing first century understandings about the spiritual world. But His actions at Caesarea Philippi and Mount Hermon, where He was basically alone with His disciples, suggest otherwise.

30. The mention of 'rough and jagged rocks' is a playful etymology of the name of Azazel. See Eibert J. C. Tigchelaar, *Prophets of Old and the Day of the End: Zechariah, the Book of Watchers, and Apocalyptic,* Brill 1995

31. 1 Enoch 13, for example, says that Azazel is bound in the rift in the desert of Dudael.

32. The Book of Enoch is once attributed (Jude 1:14) but many dozens of times it is simply quoted without citing the source. Familiar sayings such as *King of Kings and Lord of Lords,* found in both Timothy and Revelation, appear in Enoch but not in the Old Testament. See alaskandreams. net/ekklesia/Book%20of%20Enoch%20NT%20Verses. htm (accessed 17 December 2020)

33. They made their agreement by means of mutual cursing, which strongly suggests they covenanted together. One of the meanings given for Hermon is *accursed,* and the name is attributed to these angelic imprecations.

34. Also spelled Sahjaza, Semihazah, Shemihazah, Shemyazaz, Shemyaza, Sêmîazâz, Semjâzâ, Samjâzâ and Semhazah. The name Shemyaza(z) means *the name has seen* or *he sees the name* or *my name is strength*.

35. These hybrid offspring are usually the Nephilim.

36. See, for example, Michael S. Heiser, drmsh.com/naked-bible-87-exorcism-of-demons-as-part-of-the-messianic-profile/ or *The Unseen Realm: Recovering the Supernatural Worldview of the Bible*, Lexham Press 2015

37. 1 Enoch 13:7. See jstor.org/stable/3266120?seq=1

38. 1 Enoch 13:9. See jstor.org/stable/3266120?seq=1

39. An old friend testified that a panic attack can mask itself as heart attack symptoms. There is a constant rush of adrenaline. If this is not diagnosed correctly and the wrong medication prescribed, psychological issues may ensue. She testified that when her husband was given medication, he was assailed by a compulsion to commit suicide. His constant thought was simply to rush out onto the road and throw himself in front of a car.

40. 1 Enoch 6:3;6:7;10:11

41. 1 Enoch 10:4, 8

42. Kelley Coblentz Bautch, *A Study of the Geography of 1 Enoch 17–19: No One Has Seen What I Have Seen*, Brill 2003

43. With respect to the crafting of words, it should be noted that Pan was the patron deity of theatrical criticism, a literary endeavour rife with possibilities for rejection. I have twice in my life been on the receiving end of occult crafting of words. On one occasion, I was so shocked by what I read, I exclaimed, 'You don't bind people and cast them out! That's what people try to do to demons.' The shock was still so great, I repeated, 'You don't bind people and cast them out! You just don't!' Every few minutes, the initial shock recurred

and I would exclaim automatically, 'But you don't bind people and cast them out! You just don't!'

After half an hour or so, I shook myself all over and said, 'Well, I'm glad that's gone.' It was as if a binding net had been cut by my words and I was able to step out of a defilement.

44. Specifically, Akkadian.

45. Jack Mackinnon Robinson, *Christianity and Mythology*, The Rationalist Press Association, London, 1900, p 345, quoted in *Religion, Society, and Sacred Space at Banias: A Religious History of Banias/Caesarea Philippi*, 21 BC–AD 1635 by Judd H. Burton, M.A. See biblewalks.com/Files/BURTON-DISSERTATION.pdf (accessed 29 December 2020)

46. In chapters 83–84 of the Ethiopic version of the Book of Enoch, a dream is recorded about seventy shepherds, the angelic princes who are given rulership of the nations.

47. Other issues that I believe are connected with Pan are agoraphobia—which originally meant *fear of the assembly* but has come to mean *fear of open spaces*.

48. According to John Francis Wilson in *Caesarea Philippi: Banias, The Lost City of Pan*, alternate names for Pan include Min (Egyptian), Menda (Egyptian), Khem (Egyptian), Aliyan (Canaanite). The Ptolemaic rulers of Egypt had shrine to Pan which was syncretised with Khemu (also known as Min or Menda), a ram deity or goat.

Capricorn, the goat that is merged with a horse or with a sea creature, may also be a representation of Pan (considered as enthroned on a horse or a seahorse).

In the vicinity of Caesarea Philippi, there were also temples to Tyche (*fortune*), Baal Gad (*fortune*) and Baal Hermon. Gad also means *troops* and may be a play on 'gedi', *goat*, as well as *riverbank*. This latter fits the location as one of the sources of the Jordan River and explains Baal Aliyan, as both *lord of sources* and a Canaanite name for Pan.

Judd H. Burton at biblewalks.com also points out the Beth Rehob is said to be three miles east of Dan and is therefore probably Banias. This would further link the locality to the spirit of wasting, another threshold spirit.

49. Somehow derived from 'gadah' for *riverbank*.

50. Michael Brett quotes Lipinski who identifies Aliyan as the son of Baal Hammon, whom he considers equivalent to Dagon. See baal.com/?q=node/13 (accessed 26 December 2020). There is an incredible tendency for the ancient gods to all become, after a while, identified with each other—into trinities of kinds or sevenfold indistinguishable groupings. This is particularly so with the goddesses. The reason I have made the case for Pan and Azazel being essentially the same but have flagged the likelihood of difference between Azazel and Samyaza is that it's very easy to fall into the trap of mentally attributing to fallen cosmic powers the kind of Trinitarian oneness that belongs only to the Father, Son and Holy Spirit.

51. See *Hidden in the Cleft: True and False Refuge, Strategies for the Threshold #4*, the fourth book in this series

52. Luke says 'about eight' but I believe that's because, as a Gentile, he didn't realise the significance of six days in relation to the time difference between name covenants and threshold covenants. See *God's Pottery: The Sea of Names and the Pierced Inheritance* for a detailed explanation of this six-day time period between covenants.

53. Luke 9:35 AMP

54. Perhaps 'default' really doesn't give the right impression of how instantaneous this was. At one time when I was trying to overcome the false refuge of 'mental rehearsal', I had gone to Jesus and spoke to Him as He helped take down the coping mechanism I relied on when it came to injustice or rejection. I just stayed with Him until peace finally came. And then, as soon as I recognised the peace, to my total surprise, I was no longer with Jesus. I was in my false refuge. I didn't slide there or slip away gradually; the process was so fast it was as if I'd 'teleported' there. Even taking my focus off Jesus and on to the peace He provides was sufficient for the automated switches in my brain to move me to the false refuge. I learned at that time how vigilant we must be until our minds are renewed. We can't relax our guard. We want the feeling of safety that 'coping' gives us so much that, until the triggers in our minds that are so habituated to flight, fight, freezing, flattering, forestalling or forgetting are deactivated, we won't stay in that place with Jesus until the work is done.

55.   Rejection brought me into a hiding place where the temptation to wish became a double-edged trap. The spirit of wishing that I encountered was an oskmær, a *wishmaiden*, like one of the valkyries from Norse mythology who chooses the slain. These spirits haunt battlefields. I wasn't sure of that until, a few years ago, my beautician asked me to speak to her atheist husband. His worldview was coming seriously unstuck because he kept continually seeing a blue-cloaked woman—he was aware it was a spirit who followed him wherever he went and that didn't especially trouble him. What had finally spooked him was that some of his friends could see the spirit too. They would make suggestive jokes about the woman constantly sitting next to him. When he asked them to describe the woman, they all said, 'Blonde hair, dressed in blue.'

I didn't know how to communicate the idea of a valkyrie to my beautician who was Vietnamese or her husband who was a French army officer. I mentioned the word but they had no context for it. However, reminded of a story I'd heard about the killing fields of the Vietnam War, I said I'd heard rumours of 'deathmaiden' spirits who haunted the war zones. I found it fascinating that both the woman and her husband knew instantly what I was referring to. They nodded simultaneously as soon as I spoke of the 'deathmaiden'. I'd first learned about this spirit from the science fiction series, *Space: Above and Beyond*. Several segments in one episode, *Who Monitors the Birds?*, featured a spirit of death that was paradoxically both helpful and malign. It was inspired by a strange anecdote in William Manchester's *Goodbye, Darkness: A Memoir of the Pacific War.* Manchester compellingly told of revisiting various Pacific island battlefields years after the war ended, and suddenly being confronted by memories of a dark spirit surfacing with unusual clarity. The writers of *Space: Above and Beyond* used this idea and somehow managed to create just the right imagery, despite the vagueness of Manchester's description. One of the guest stars, on coming on to the set of *Who Monitors the Birds?* and seeing the actress made up as the spirit of Death, was enough taken aback to say, 'I saw you in 'Nam.'

56. It may be significant that 'Azazel' is a head rhyme, more common in Hebrew poetry than tail rhyme, with 'azab' and 'izzabon', *wares* or *trading*.

57. The Hebrew word for these magic pillows is 'keseth'. The word rhymes with 'qeseth', the *pouch* or *inkhorn* which contains the instrument to mark the foreheads of those who are to be saved. The qeseth is clearly like a phylactery which was worn on the forehead, and which had similar connotations of a sign showing who was to be saved. (In this, it was like a mezuzah, the doorposts or pillars of a doorway, which was both a memorial—an aid to memory—and a witness.)

The magic pillows (or pouches) were thus counterfeits and were for soul-hunting rather than soul-saving. There may be some connection between these pillows and the 'ob', *wineskin, skinbottle*, that is also a word for a *necromancer, medium, spiritist*, or *a person with familiar spirit*. Related to 'ob' is "ow', 'uw', or 'o', meaning *desire, wish, water-carrier*, and perhaps *revenant*. The relationship between a skin and a familiar spirit is found in the Norse concept of the skinchanger with its overtones of witchcraft.

58.   pitt.edu/~dash/nightmare.html (accessed 4 January 2021)

59.   I put 'pandemic' and 'vaccine' in quote marks because, until recently, these words were understood very differently from today. Before 2020, a 'pandemic' had to have a sizeable mortality rate as well as a wide distribution across a country or around the world. Less than one quarter of one percent of the world's population dying of any disease would not have qualified in the past. And just over two percent of those contracting the disease, the mortality rate at the time of writing, would not have either.

Also in the past, a 'vaccine' was understood to offer old-style immunity to a disease, not to simply alleviate the symptoms. When a 'vaccine' becomes what, in the past, was just a 'treatment', then old-fashioned treatments are increasingly excluded, as has happened in this year of fear. I say 'old-style' because immunity today is becoming defined in terms of the percentage of the population who have received a vaccine, not the ability of a person to combat a particular infection, either because of natural resistance or because they have caught the infection and have recovered.

60.   See *God's Pottery: The Sea of Names and the Pierced Inheritance*, Armour Books 2016

61.   Derek Prince in *Rediscovering God's Church: How can you fulfil your calling for the 21st century?* says the closest translation for 'ekklesia', the word used by Jesus to describe His church, is 'knesset', the name given to the Israeli parliament.

62.   We usually think it's faith but, as I have indicated in *Dealing with Python*, the first book in this series, that's a common mistake. Even Paul of Tarsus made this error when he was in Philippi but, by the time he got to Corinth, he had realised what the truth was.

63. See *God's Panoply: The Armour of God and the Kiss of Heaven*, Armour Books 2016.

64. It's also spelled the same as 'uzzah', suggesting not just *strength* but *goat*.

65. The rules involving hair and the covering of the head are among the most perilous areas in Scripture. They are quicksand, given that there are exceptions even within the commandments of God, let alone cultural exceptions. The Nazarite vow is such an exception. For some people, dreadlocks are not a statement of rebellion against society at all; it is a matter of spiritual empowerment.

66. When Samson died, it was between two pillars—again a parallel to the gates he stole with their pillars.

67. TE Dowling wrote: 'In the 19th century, the city of Gaza declined. The Jews that were concentrated there were mostly barley merchants. They bartered with the Bedouins for barley, which they exported to the beer breweries of Europe.'

'The trade and commerce of Gaza are almost exclusively confined to the gathering in and exportation of barley, which is grown on the plain of Philistia, and in the neighbourhood of Beersheba. The majority of the inhabitants of the city and district obtain their livelihood from this trade alone. The widespread olive-grove to the north and north-east, however, creates a considerable manufacture of soap, which Gaza exports in large quantities... Gaza is in a state of lethargy for about nine months out of twelve, until the middle of April, when the barley crop is cut, because most of the inhabitants earn their living by the barley trade. In consequence of much idleness during this slack period, drunkenness is not an uncommon vice. The wealthy merchants buy at harvest-time large quantities of barley, which are generally exported or stored, until the prices in Great Britain and Egypt are high, when they sell to British and other purchasers. The poorer traders pitch small tents in the neighbourhood of the city, and among the Bedouins, to whom they sell clothes, sweets, coffee, and other articles, taking barley in exchange. When they have secured a sufficient amount, they sell it either to the agents of the European merchants, or to the native merchants of the city. Anyone who visits Gaza in June and July will be astonished to see the large quantities of barley heaped upon the sea-shore, awaiting the arrival of steamers.' See *Gaza: A City of Many Battles (From The Family of Noah to the Present Day)*, Theodore Edward Dowling, D.D. Archdeacon in Syria; Canon of St. George's Collegiate Church, Jerusalem; Commissary For Eastern Church Intercourse Within The Anglican Bishopric In Jerusalem, published under the direction of *The Tract Committee London Society For Promoting Christian Knowledge* Northumberland Avenue, W.C.; 43, Queen Victoria Street, E.C. Brighton: 129, North Street, New York: E.S. Gorham 1913

68. Tel Azzaziyat is nearby and may be another reference to Azazel encoded in the landscape. Caesarea Philippi had many shrines and temples, including one to the Emperor Augustus and another to Roma. Tyche, goddess of fortune, was at one time the patron of the city and coins to her have been found, dressed in military style with rudder and cornucopia. Caesarea Philippi was briefly renamed 'Neronias' after the Emperor Nero, but this didn't last long and was changed as soon as Nero's memory became condemned in Rome.

It was well-known amongst the Jews that the Gentiles syncretised Pan and Yahweh. Coins to Pan have been found at Caesarea Philippi. The images show Pan holding a staff, making it easily identifiable as an item of idolatrous tribute. According to contemporary rabbis, coins which featured figures with birds, a staff, an orb or a similar device in their hands were picturing idols. (See John Francis Wilson, *Caesarea Philippi: Banias, The Lost City of Pan*, I.B. Tauris, 2004)

The mythic figure known as the Green Elijah of the Druze (and Muslims), also called Al-Khidr, is still revered in this vicinity. Some stories of Al-Khidr and Merlin the magician have obviously influenced one another. Many churches dedicated to St. George in the Holy Land and surrounding nations were originally shrines to Al-Khidr.

Caesarea Philippi is, for Jews, the only place in Israel where one may recite the blessing 'who uproots idolatry in our land.' See religionunplugged.com/news/2020/7/29/st-peter-and-pan-grotto-and-spring-in-the-golan-heights-is-revered-by-christians-and-druze-but-reviled-as-pagan-cult-center-by-jews (accessed 4 January 2021)

69. These games were held at Berytus, Rome and Caesarea Philippi. See Will Durant, *Caesar and Christ*, quoted in padfield.com/acrobat/history/Caesarea_Philippi.pdf (accessed 4 Jan 2021)

70. 'It is remarkable that the first city builders were descendants of Cain. City builders are also named among the descendants of the cursed Ham. Israel was a nation of shepherds and farmers. Jerusalem is also a large city, of course, but the prophet says that Jerusalem will be inhabited as a town without walls. Massing people together leads to a lot of injustice. The present world cities are a living proof of this, with their murders, theft, debauchery and smog—human anthills, urban jungles, where the law of the fittest rules.' Willem Glashouwer, *Behold He Comes*

71. That case is also deeply infiltrated by the activity of the spirit of abuse.

72. Esau was called Edom, *red*. Does this indicate the sun's redness? Jacob's most significant encounters with God were at night; perhaps suggesting the twins were as day and night.

Esau was hairy but other evocations in his name may perhaps have led him to also be called Seir, *hairy, goat*.

These are ez, *goat*, and oz, *strength* (as in Boaz)—and Esau was definitely a man who relied on his own strength in hunting game and pleasing his father.

73. The 'Black Land' was the name the Egyptians called their own country.

74. Again this story is one deeply infiltrated by the activity of the spirit of abuse. I certainly don't want to give the impression by the shortness of this summary that Jonathan's actions can be excused in any way. There are hints in the Hebrew that he was a vicious, opportunistic man—a total contrast to his meek grandfather. See *God's Priority: World-Mending and Generational Testing*, Armour Books 2017

75. From the podcast, jeremiah-johnson.mykajabi.com/products/purifying-the-prophetic-e-course

76. That is, the non-human dead spirits resulting from the coupling between angels and humanity, who continually seek to be re-embodied in flesh.

77. The astrological symbol of Capricorn (21 December to 21 January) begins close to the solstice connected with Tropic of Capricorn. Since a solstice is a threshold marker for the seasons, this suggests an ancient understanding of Pan's connection with time thresholds.

78. For people of British and Celtic ancestry, Bran and the legends about him are almost certainly more significant than those of Pan or Azazel. The link between the mythologies is not an obvious one. However so many Christian writers make it instinctively, I don't doubt it is correct. Pan was worshipped in Rome at Lupercalia from 13–15 February. The rites of Lupercalia were to avert evil spirits and purify the city, through the sacrifices of goats and a dog and the offering of cakes. There was also a fertility rite in which the goatskin-clad priests, the Luperci—or *brothers of the wolf*—would strike women

who wish to conceive. The date naturally connects with Valentine's Day—an early Christian saint reputedly beheaded for his faith. This provides the link to Bran the Wonderful Head. I would like to be able to find a less tenuous link than this, but at the moment, it's what I have.

The name 'Bran' has a variety of meanings—originally it was most likely *raven* (or perhaps the *alder* tree) but at some point it came to be associated with *wrens* and *robins*. Mythically speaking, robins are connected to Robin Hood and his Merrie Men. According to Robert Graves, the Merrie Men were originally Morris Dancers who participated in a fertility ritual, disguised as animals— they were considered satyrs or fauns. In the ritual, the 'robin' was killed by the 'jack'. On the evening before the dance, an orgy took place and nine months afterwards, the children born as a result of the couplings on that night were often given the name to indicate their biological parentage: 'Robinson', 'Jackson' or 'Morrison'. This aspect of Bran as well as Robin Hood not only connects back to Pan as a satyr but also to the lust aspect of Azazel.

The importance of Bran in the national life of Britain persists even today. Bran 'the Wonderful Head' is considered the national guardian of Britain. His head was said to have been buried at the White Mount in London, which later became the White Tower, and still later the Tower of London. There the Head protects Britain against invasion, just as Pan was said to have protected Greece from invasion by the Persians. Although King Arthur was supposed to have dug up the Head so people would rely on Camelot for protection, Bran has reasserted his prominence in the last century. His symbol, the raven, is considered to be evidence of his presence and it is said that, if ever ravens disappear from the Tower of London, then the nation is in dire peril. This was taken seriously enough during World War II that Winston Churchill allegedly ordered the wings of the ravens at the Tower clipped so they couldn't fly away. This wing-clipping

continues to the present-day. (standard.co.uk/news/
london/tower-of-london-s-queen-raven-missing-feared-
dead-b872986.html accessed 16 January 2021)

An old British tradition involves stoning wrens and
robins on 26 December—Boxing Day. The reasons are
lost in the mists of time but it is clear that this is a specific
date when Bran has particular power. (atlanticreligion.
com/2014/11/09/the-pagan-roots-of-st-martins-day-
11th-november/)

In Painswick in Gloucestershire, a group of 18th-century
gentry, led by Benjamin Hyett, organised an annual
procession dedicated to Pan, during which a statue of
the deity was held aloft, and people shouted 'Highgates!
Highgates!' Hyett also erected temples and follies to Pan
in the gardens of his house and a 'Pan's lodge', located over
Painswick Valley. The tradition died out in the 1830s, but
was revived in 1885 by the new vicar, W.H. Seddon, who
mistakenly believed that the festival had been ancient
in origin. One of Seddon's successors, however, was less
appreciative of the pagan festival and put an end to it in
1950, when he had Pan's statue buried.

Other English appreciations of Pan have included the
seventh chapter of Kenneth Grahame's *The Wind in the
Willows* which features an unnamed numinous nature
entity, identified only as *The Piper at the Gates of Dawn*.
Pink Floyd's debut studio album has the same name.

For some reason, *The Wind in the Willows* is not the only
children's story to mute the wildness of Pan. Peter Pan is
another. So, apparently is the Pied Piper: 'Whether it is
the disturbing guise of the Pied Piper of the thirteenth-
century town of Hamelin in Lower Saxony or the original
Greek god Pan, panic can sweep through people and
hurl them towards death whether by war, illness, or a
sustainable future denied. Recall: 'the Piper advanced and
the children followed, / And when all were in to the very

last, / The door in the mountain-side shut fast.' (Robert Browning, *The Pied Piper of Hamelin: A Child's Story*).

And while we're recalling literature, it's worth remembering the chaos that ensued when HG Well's *The War of the Worlds* was dramatised and first aired over the radio. Known to history as the 'Panic Broadcast', it combined several aspects of Pan's agenda: panic, war, confusion and even, in its aftermath, theatrical criticism. The chaos and confusion of this connect back to Bel the Confounder (or Confuser) who was worshipped at Babylon (Babel).

Early Christians were encouraged by a story that circulated in the first century about Pan. Plutarch, the first century Greek historian who was also the high priest at the temple of Python Apollo in Delphi, recorded the tale of Thamus, a sailor who was on his way to Italy. As the ship passed the island of Paxi, a voice hailed him and said, 'Thamus, are you there? When you reach Palodes, take care to proclaim that the great god Pan is dead.' Thamus obeyed this direction and the news was greeted from the shore with lamenting cries. Because this event was reported to have occurred sometime during the reign of the Emperor Tiberius—who ruled from 14–37 AD—Christian apologists across the millennia since have seen significance in the timing. These are the years of Jesus' adulthood, ministry and death as well as the early days of the church. During the Middle Ages, the 'death of Pan' was understood as the death of all demons—since one interpretation of Pan is *all*—and thus the end of the old pagan order and the beginning of the new. Pan might have died in the first century but people have been trying to revive his worship ever since.

79. One such demi-god who was associated with both rejection and hair was Maui.

80. For example, binding and silencing a person, rather than a demon. Shunning or casting out a person is antithetical

to the teachings of Jesus. If you have been bound and silenced, shunned or cast out, it is wise to remove yourself totally from those practising this kind of abuse. When a person is dominated by the spirit of abuse, we have Scriptural sanction to take ourselves out of harm's way.

81. By 'old-style' immunity, I mean the sort of immunity a person developed from natural exposure to disease, not the new definition of 'immunity' which means 'vaccinated'.

82. For those of a mathematical bent, 2.1% of 1.1% is less than a quarter of one percent. It *might* be *epi*demic but, in the strictest linguistic sense, it's not *pan*demic.

83. Another way of expressing this is the leadership principle: look to the practices, not to the individual.

84. Mark 10:18 NASB

85. Make no mistake about how common this is in today's world. There are various ways this happens.

   1. Some believers park their own views above the plain reading of Scripture; they have an evolutionary view of humanity's understanding of God. But this is crowning yourself, rather than the hero. Installing yourself as king has happened since time immemorial. However, in the evolutionary view, humanity is crowned as the hero.

   2. Some believers create a Scriptural hierarchy. Some consider that the Old Testament has nothing to teach us. Yet, how can we understand the significance of what Jesus does at Caesarea Philippi unless we grasp that it has to do with Azazel and atonement? Some believers further consider that the writings of Paul take precedence over the words of Jesus—because Paul is post-resurrection and the gospels are pre-resurrection. Others read with the hero, not with the text and so present us with idealised men whose shortcomings are airbrushed out of commentaries

so that they become virtual prototypes of perfection. These Scriptural heroes become the role models for today's leaders. But there is only one true hero in Scripture: it's Jesus, no one else.

86.   John 6:32 BSB

87.   Pastor Ivor Myers points out that Uzzah was trying to prevent the Ark dropping to the ground, which would have been a rebuke to all of Israel. He was trying to stop a message of rebuke from God from reaching its intended audience. See youtube.com, *Let it Drop! The Trouble with Uzzah's Infamous Act*

88.   Ted Peters, *Sin: Radical Evil in Soul and Society*, Wm. B. Eerdmans Publishing, 1994

89.   *Dealing with Resheph: Spirit of Trouble—Strategies for the Threshold #6.* Since writing that book, I have found further indications that Jesus honoured the household of Saul in his interactions with Mary, Martha and Lazarus.

90.   This includes the covenant of peace. I believe that the covenant of freedom (Jeremiah 34:8) is another name for a threshold covenant. However, I may be wrong. I do not believe that the so-called 'sandal covenant' is a covenant, since it seems to me to be a contract that lacks the primary aspect of oneness that would distinguish it as a covenant. The same is true for the so-called 'covenant of the tithe'—I believe here that an obligation of covenant has been misinterpreted as the covenant itself. And, although I agree the marriage covenant is indeed a covenant, I do not think—at least at this time—that it is a separate covenant in its own right. Rather, I see it as a combination of covenants.

91.   In particular, the *Zohar*, the foundational text of the *Kabbalah*—which, unfortunately, rapidly degenerated into an occult text.

92. Isaiah 34:14 mentions a satyr/goat (which may be Azazel) along with Lilith and 'ijim', *jackals*. The howling of jackals is connected with *desire:* 'owh' or ''wh' is *howl*, 'owh' is also *jackal* or *falcon*, ''wh' is *desire, wish* or *covet*, but can also be *tenderly inclined*. Other words for *jackal* suggest links to Leviathan ('tan', *sea monster*), to hell ('shual', *desire, Sheol*) and to Ziz, the spirit of forgetting (tangentially through 'zeeb', *wolf*). See also Endnote 57.

93. In my previous books, I called this the 'Janissary spirit' because at the time I was not able to discern the Scriptural name for this threshold entity. I don't want to completely sideline that term because it brings out an otherwise hidden agenda. I believe that Belial can be imaged as a goat like Azazel, and that it is probably lord of the 'shedim', *goat demons*, that Israel was forbidden to worship.

94. The Greek word 'tragoidia', meaning *tragedy,* stems from 'tragos', *goat,* for the songs sung at goat sacrifices to Dionysus. The Romans also worshiped Dionysus as Bacchus, who often disguised himself as a goat. Bronze goats covered in gold leaf were placed in vineyards to encourage fertility. The goat symbolized lightning in Greece, China, Tibet, and elsewhere. The Hebrews wove the cloth of the tabernacle out of goat hair to symbolize the lightning that appeared on Mount Sinai at the appearance of God. (See:base.dnsgb.com.ua/files/book/Agriculture/ Animal-Agriculture/The-Encyclopedia-of-Historic-and-Endangered-Livestock.pdf, accessed 10 January 2021)

95. Though there may be death magic involved.

96. Mahalath (also called Basemath) was the daughter of Ishmael and the sister of Nebaioth, who is believed to be the progenitor of the Nabataeans. This great trading nation of nomadic Arabs established their capital at Petra between two and four centuries before Christ. They are thought to have displaced the Edomites, however, if they are descended from Nebaioth, the firstborn son of Ishmael, this may simply be their ancestral homeland.

Not far from Petra is 'Little Petra', more properly Beida, which is believed to be the location of the spring which Ishmael's mother found and where she had an encounter with God at Beer-Lahai-Roi, *the well of the Living One who sees me*. The ruined village here is Chai, *living*, and its well Ein el-Chai, *well of life* or *well of the living one.* David Ben-Gad HaCohen, in line with ancient authorities, suggests that it not only fits the description in Genesis but further proposes that this is the Kadesh of the wilderness wanderings (to be distinguished from Kadesh Barnea, a different location.) He also suggests that this is the place that Isaac gave to Esau as his 'territory' when Isaac blessed him after being tricked by Jacob. If this was the case, it seems that Esau, very wisely, secured the 'territorial rights' by marrying into the only other family who might have a claim on the area—the family of Ishmael. (thetorah.com/article/locating-beer-lahai-roi – accessed 22 January 2021)

97.   Perhaps the inspiration for this came from Leviticus 14:1–7 which is a kind of 'scape-bird' ritual.

98.   See *Dealing with Leviathan: Spirit of Retaliation*, the fifth book in this series.

99.   When people do become free of rules or mind control, they often acquire the belief that, if others are still obeying the rules or following a tradition, they must have a 'religious spirit'. The possibility that the others are utilising their freedom to submit to a particular way does not often occur to the newly escaped. A genuine religious spirit involves separation, sacrifice and sorcery.

100.   On Yom Kippur, the lamb was tied to the altar and inspected to see if it was flawless. The High Priest pressed the lamb to put the sins of the people on it. This laying on of hands imparted the weight of sin to the lamb, which was then slain. At 3 o'clock, the high priest shouted 'It is finished', caught the blood of the lamb in a vessel and shook it as he ran from the altar into the most Holy Place, yelling, 'Do not touch me!'

101. See Judges 18:30.

102. Dunedin Multidisciplinary Health & Development Study.

103. 94% are still taking part at the time of writing, nearly a half century later. The original 'year' went from 1 April 1972 to 31 March 1973.

104. One of the most alarming aspects of some current Christian movements is the re-definition of the word *repentance* to mean we should *always agree swiftly and humbly with any accusations of the enemy*. Although, in this instance where Jesus is confronting the devil, there are no accusations (though there might be some implied in '*if* You are the Son of God'), I believe the principle applies that we should never agree with the enemy. If we sense accusations from any threshold, we should turn to our advocate and paraclete, the Holy Spirit, and ask: 'What do You think about that? Is it right?' Our agreement should always be with the Spirit of Truth, never the Father of Lies.

105. A penname for the author Margaret Barber.

106. This word is 'suph', *reeds*, which is very similar to 'saph', *threshold*. Another word is 'qaneh', which is the possible source of Cana, the name of the town where Jesus performed His first miracle. A 'first' is always a threshold event.

107. See base.dnsgb.com.ua/files/book/Agriculture/ Animal-Agriculture/The-Encyclopedia-of-Historic-and-Endangered-Livestock.pdf (accessed 10 January 2021).

108. The word for *fear* in this verse is 'deilia' from 'deilos', *timidity, cowardliness, fearfulness*. It is related to the Aramaic word, 'dechal', *slink*; which in turn links to Hebrew 'zachal', *worm-like, serpent-like, crawling with fear*. Fear is not only a tactic of Pan the satyr and Azazel, the scapegoat. It is also a tactic of the threshold guardians who are imaged as serpents, such as Python and Leviathan.

109. See theculturetrip.com/europe/united-kingdom/ northern-ireland/articles/how-did-the-shankill-road-become-northern-irelands-most-notorious-street/ (accessed 22 January 2021)

110. This story was originally told by Jane Bentley and Neil Paynter in *Around a Thin Place: An Iona Pilgrimage Guide*, Wild Goose Resource Group 2011

111. We always have a split second in which to turn to God. He designed us that way. The amygdala is primary place in our brains for processing fear (and other strong negative emotions, such as rage). Normally the cortex processes input, but it can get short-circuited in cases of extreme stress. The information then goes to the amygdala.

In *The Word for Today*, Bob Gass explains: 'In between your brain's intake and your body's response time, there's what researchers call the "life-giving quarter-second". And that quarter-second—although it doesn't sound very long—is huge...That quarter-second is the time when the Holy Spirit can take control. That's when you can choose to give the foothold to the Holy Spirit, or you can give it to sin.' (6 August 2020) See also:

brainmadesimple.com/amygdala.html

study.com/academy/lesson/the-amygdala-definition-role-function.html

psychologytoday.com/blog/i-got-mind-tell-you/ 201508/the-amygdala-is-not-the-brains-fear-center

If you found this book helpful, other books in this series may prove useful too as you address the issues that bar your way into your calling:

Dealing with Ziz:

Spirit of Forgetting

Strategies for the Threshold #2

The most significant threshold point of life is the doorway into God's unique calling for us. He invites us through covenant to fulfil the destiny we were born to achieve.

However, many of us fall at the threshold, rather than pass over it. We experience constriction, wasting, retaliation and forgetting—to such a degree it's easy to doubt the promises of God.

Dealing with Ziz examines the spiritual implications of forgetting in relation to threshold covenants. Since the opposite of remembering is dismembering—dismembering of truth—the spirit of forgetting is able to block access to our calling.

Yet there is an answer, a Fruit of the Spirit that overcomes Ziz.

If you're wondering how to overcome the issues of the threshold and the associated ngodly covenants, this book has the answer. Other books help you recognise the problem, this one points out the first step on the path.

Hidden in the Cleft:

True and False Refuge

Strategies for the Threshold #4

Jesus had a refuge—a safe haven—He retreated to when His life was in danger.

What does His choice reveal about where best to find sanctuary in times of trouble? What is the significance of the hiding place He used for an entire season? How can we discern the difference between a true and false refuge?

Removal of our false refuges is the first step towards achieving our life's calling—the divine purpose for which God created us. Yet all too often we fail to recognise how we've defaulted to a false refuge when disappointment strikes.

This book offers practical help, hope and encouragement towards achieving your destiny in Christ.

Dealing with Leviathan:

Spirit of Retaliation

Strategies for the Threshold #5

Retaliation, reprisal, retribution—many of us express the ferocity of our encounters with the spirit of Leviathan with such words. Most believers are stunned by savagery of the backlash they experience, and are baffled by God's seeming failure to intervene.

Reparation, recompense, restitution, restoration—these promised corrections to injustice are smashed just as they seem within reach. Why does this happen?

As we examine Scripture, we find that Leviathan is an officer of God's royal court. When we violate the consecration of that Holy Place, it has the legal right to remove us. It does not do so gently.

Dealing with Leviathan offers insight into overcoming this spirit of the deep.

Dealing with Resheph:

Spirit of Trouble

Strategies for the Threshold #6

Resheph is mentioned seven times in Scripture. A fallen seraph and throne guardian, it is identified here as a hidden face of Leviathan, the spirit that counterattacks against dishonour. Symbolised as a stag and an archer, Resheph is connected with flames and fire, fever, financial distress, mental illness, drought and scorching heat as well as the underworld.

Jesus warred against this spirit at least seven times. It's easy to miss these battles because it's easy to miss the prophecies Jesus was fulfilling and the mention of Resheph associated with them.

This is a companion volume to *Dealing With Leviathan* and examines the obstacles we face on the threshold into our calling.

influencing or being influenced

God, let these lessons not be
Wasted, use this pain for
Your purpose.

How many times have you been
rejected in life? pp/135

9 781925 380293